The Q

G000090706

Harry Steel

chipmunkapublishing

the mental health publisher

Published by

Chipmunkapublishing

PO Box 6872

Brentwood

Essex CM13 1ZT

United Kingdom

http://www.chipmunkapublishing.com

Chipmunkapublishing gratefully acknowledge the support of Arts Council England.

Biography

Harry was born in a British Military Hospital in Germany in 1968. Harry`s childhood was mainly being brought up in a children's home, of which his parents owned. Being treated just the same as all the other children in care, Harry had good, and bad times growing up in those years, just like most childhoods.

Harry`s life changed dramatically when he started his journey experiment with street drugs.

The first out of his mind experience was when he was shown how to inhale butane gas. He found the buzz to be incredible. When Harry was old enough, like most teenagers, he started on the booze. Then Harry tried pot... and booze, then LSD...and booze, then LSD, booze and pot, then LSD, booze, pot and amphetamines...then Ecstasy...then cocaine...and then...well, you know the rest. Harry`s mind set had now started a downward spiral.

Harry knew the drink and drugs had taken their toll, however, tried his best to ignore the illness that he had now accentuated, and of course, he had now become his own worst enemy, a paranoid enemy. Having at that time an undiagnosed natural illness of manic depression, mixed with drug abuse, Harry had now taken a dark turning.

By the time Harry was thirty years of age, he had managed to abuse his mind to the extent where if he didn`t change, then there may never have been a way home.

Overcoming his paranoia and depressions was Harry`s hardest task of all, but of course, this was an action that would inevitably save himself, from himself.

Now that the street drugs are in the far distant past, he`s learnt to manage his mind, he now embraces it in the same way a parent embraces their children, with love and tenderness. Harry wrote this novel with memories of a troubled and over-active mind, these times have now passed, he has released himself by way of his words, writing was a part of the cure.

Harry Steel

Foreword

The first thing I want to say, is that this novel I have written is **not** a self help piece for others, nor is it a biography, it's just thoughts, words, and my novel...nothing more. This novel is from the mindset of me when I was struggling to get through, in language I understand. That doesn't mean to say that other persons looking for a way to understand themselves shouldn't write, I strongly suggest that they do, as I have found writing to be an exceptional release of tension.

My novel is a piece of fiction, however, it's written from the viewpoint of someone who felt confined, confined by the combination of natural illnesses of manic depression, mild bi-polar, dyslexia and of course the abuse of street drugs. This was a highly destructive cocktail. I dissected all actions and thoughts, my own, and other peoples, often ending with the wrong conclusion...which was not healthy.

The first chapter within the novel is in fact the tenth. It carries the 'C' word. This word is only used once within the entire novel, and it is used in this chapter. If you can handle the first chapter as an 'In your face' piece...then I hope the rest will flow.

The second chapter is the first chapter, it's the beginning...'The arrival' and if you're wondering why I put the tenth chapter in first...again...it's because if you're offended by strong words and graphic images...then this isn't a novel for you.

My novel revolves completely around one man who waits in a queue. The read goes through his mindset of anger, frustration, and fantasy enhanced by a wild imagination.

'The arrival' chapter deals with an analysing state of mind, which wanders into an aggressive state, then back to analysing one's own frustrations. For someone such as myself, this was a constant state of mind, there was never continuity. However, my late Nan's words always rung in my head..."Food for thought son"...and she was right.

The chapter 'Geezer' is a fictional piece that deals with irony.

My story regarding Mack the washed out bounty hunter is a piece of fiction that evolved with my imagination. Mack being a bounty hunter, deaths, memories, villas being blown up with a growing awareness of his placid side, again, are all a work of my imagination.

As for the chapter regarding 'The twins' again...how the mind wanders.

The chapter regarding 'Clever Girl' is a lengthy one that involves another exaggerated and fictitious piece. It's a tale of a betrayal of trust, of all involved.

To fuse the novel together a robbery takes place, this is where the characters wait, as to where the queue stands, and of course the last chapter, is to open the book...as such.

The reader should gain an insight into how a restricted persons mind may wander...and open one's thoughts regarding. These restrictions when it comes down to mental health issues are sometimes enhanced by *some* of those people around them, because of their insatiable desire to cause injustice, which of course in turn does nothing to help the person with the issues. In my mind to overcome ones illness regarding what I have wrote here, avoiding people who are unjust or negative towards these situations...helps. I was going to name the novel 'Frustration' but it sounded too much like a game one would buy for the kids at Christmas.

A wheelchair is obvious, and easy to understand. A mind is not so obvious, and not so easy to understand, empathy rather than sympathy.

The Novel needs to be read from cover to cover, not missing any words, the reader may lose the plot if pieces are missed.

In addition, some of my words are harsh to say the least, but if I hadn't written it like this...I wouldn't have written them at all...no apologies.

I would like to take this opportunity to thank Jason Pegler (A can of Madness) and CO of Chipmunka, who in talking with via email in the beginning stages of this publication, has, I feel, helped me a great deal in understanding my own writing, which in turn has brought me further in understanding myself. Also to Paul Kirven and the gang at Chipmunka, who have worked hard on publishing this novel, many thanks.

I hope all those who read my work enjoy it.

Harry Steel

Harry Steel

Chapter 1
The Danube Basin
Day 3

The sea vixens roared from over a mile away as they faded into the distance, returning to the Ark Royal.

Going over the ridge of the basin, looking into the bowl, the glow of stubble, what's left of the crop, brightens with a glow of solitude as the wind blows brashly over – nature not giving a second thought.

Not a sound from feet, breath, hardware, nothing. Just the stench of Napalm. The stench of gel mixed with the fuel and JP-5...bad fucking news.

A smouldering mess of unrecognisable pieces. Annihilation. The smell's unbearable. The Radfan rebels have gone. White compounded mud bricks, other shit which made up the village and the community – black, dormant, burnt, scattered, truly fucking done. The still coma of death surrounds every sense, getting into every pore.

No bodies. The Radfan rebels knew we were coming, looks like they've been gone for a long time. Absolute anni-fuckin-hilation. The Yemen boarder, they've gone there.

Something's not right here. Something ... is so not fucking right here.

A smell, not Napalm. What the fuck is it? Where the fuck's that smell coming from?

All clear, I know it's all fucking clear you cunt, I just fucking told you that. Fucking hand signals, not fucking smoky arm signals, o-fucking-kay!

Ghost walking up to the top of a brick well, the smell's getting stronger, something ain't fuuuuckiiiiing riiiiiiight ...

A draw of breath, like he's just surfaced from deep water, pours into Mack's mouth. The sheets are soaked. He's drenched. The electric fuzz ... the echo of his brain coming to its senses, it's all too much.

Mack sits on the side of his bed, elbows on knees with his head in his hands, crying like a deeply torn soul. The visions of those dead villagers down the well ... children. Mack's angry. Mack is so angry. He still can't comprehend why they did that. They could have polluted the wells some other way. The eyeballs in his sockets thrash from side to side as the fury grows. Mack wants to release his anger.

Starting with that fucking chair against the door. *The bed goes upside down. The phone wrenched from its socket goes through the window. The wardrobe doors ripped from their hinges, forced into the shower cubicle, smashing the mirror and shower head with a crash to wake. A cabinet, stormed against the wall, disintegrating into three chunky pieces...*

Visions of terror in the child's eye almost demands the command to scream through his blood-shot tear-soaked eyes. His rampage won't go outside his mind or body; it's not allowed to. Restraining his inner matter, bringing his forecast actions to a halt, he looks around at the untouched room, knowing that *their* pain, is over.

This somehow gives a relief from the anger, as he knows that peace and tranquillity will also be his ... one day.

Mack gets his shit together and runs a shower, he just hopes no one pisses him off today. *Fuck it!!!*

Chapter 2

The arrival

I've just arrived at this place and looking around at the brightly lit area, I guess it's about three-by-three square metres, wall shelves jam-packed with products – things to exchange for cash, a cheque, or even plastic.

The suspended ceiling illuminates the room with sunken lights, square, with the dull shadows of dead insects lying on the topside of the glass. A quiet din weighs in the room, but people *do* seem interested in what's for sale. Slowly browsing, picking up bubble wrapped goods, looking at the price, then putting them back. Cards on a white metal swivel stand always seem to attract the women, especially the older ones. They're the ones that have a book full of birthday dates, christenings, weddings, hospital appointments, and all those things that need cards. It involves them in the occasion, occasions in other people's lives, it's a way to keep themselves busy and unforgotten, I suppose – and of course, they do it because they're thoughtful.

Not like the *working* man though, who only has time for *work,* and maybe a pint afterwards. He doesn't have time to browse card displays, reading the inner words while judging the picture to suss out its suitability for the engagement ahead. No, the *working* man just has to turn up to those engagements when they're told to do so, by their spouses, relatives, or friends. In addition of course they must be on their best behaviour, but all the while not really wanting to be there at all. Yep, they're thinking of their mates having a laugh down the local boozer, or at the footie match, there's no airs and graces there.

I've come to the conclusion that this place stinks. However, I don't have a choice about being here, but if I did have the choice, I wouldn't be, just like all the other blokes my age who are working or doing more manlike things.

There's always a collective when I come to this place, but today there's a different kind. A few of them I recognise from years gone by...and others I would *like* to have remembered from years gone by. My mind is my companion...my closest companion.

Two girls stand in front of me. They *have* to be identical twins, they're both wearing flat black sensible leather-upper shoes, they seem joined at the hip, so close it's like they've never even sneezed without each other being there. Which makes me notice the tilled floor carpet, looking like it's a million years old. Dried flattened chewing gum sticks to it in grey flat blobs over the worn-out red-and-blue chequered pattern. In front of them, there's a mix of male, female, old, young, fat, bald, a couple, and another couple with a baby, a single mother, and two fat idiots acting like they own the place, as they shove their sweaty glutinous bodies around, making space for their overfed egos.

Most are like me, waiting impatiently to get to the front. This is a queue that doesn't boast excitement and that's a fact. I'm a little rushed today and can see it could take anything up to twenty minutes or so to get served. As long as the rest of the people in the queue busy things along and don't faff, then all around should be well. If there's one thing that really gets my back up, it's faffers! *Especially* when I'm in a rush.

The walls are yellow, what a crap colour to paint a post office. Is this colour supposed to make me feel better about waiting or something? In does infact do the opposite, especially when the pillars are chipped and knackered with the grey flaky plaster showing through its old and over-painted exterior, and all the while, I have to listen to *stupid* music from the 80s. I wonder why they play this music? Is it for soothing purposes? Or is it supposed to make us all start dancing and for some sort of ritual humanistic amalgamation process to start? Again it does the opposite, what it is doing though, is winding me up even more!

Looking longingly at the counter where we'll soon be served, I see the attendants who work behind the paranoid knife-proof glass, as they condescendingly smile at whoever needs their assistance. Probably because they do a job that demands protection, importance flashes in their eyes as they serve the next customer. I know how they look, I also know how they feel, they're not *really* wanting to be there, they're looking forward to the next tea break and home time as much as anyone, but they don't want to show it, because then they'd be the same as the rest of us, wouldn't they? However, they have to earn the pennies just like everyone else, we all have mouths to feed, haven't we?

I can only just see their faces because of a barrage of obstructive advertising that some idiot companies have taken the initiative to waste time and money on, whose dreams are they this time? Whose dreams will soon be breaking into pieces this time, because of the rent, the rates, the overheads, staff wages, and all that stuff that comes with a small business? Those greedy, crippling, extortionate business bills will help crush their dreams, just as they crushed the ones before them, the ones who excitedly set their sights on paying the mortgage off early, paving a way to buying a yacht, owning their own private jet and being king-don at the Vegas limelight. Yes, they were there at those very same premises...with the very same dream, only a little while ago.

Think about it, why did the premises become vacant in the first place? And don't be fobbed off with the story about the last tenants moving to larger premises...because that's the oldest golden carrot in the book. However, having said that, they *still* managed to sell the lease to another dream...didn't they? Oh, and the banks, they love it don't they?

"Is there anything else I can help you with while you're here? We do insurances now if you're interested?" the greedy bankers offer.

What...am I going on a bit too long about all this?...I can't help it...they prey on the dream the optimist has. They survive on those dreams, don't they? Oh, they'll have had their fare share of the proprietor's dreams...in the way of sweat, hard work, and hard earned currency. Oh yes, don't you know? The bank charges and hidden fees will play their part in ripping a little more flesh from the already stumbling animal...*won't* they?

There's so much of this idiot advertising that reading it almost makes me laugh out loud. I couldn't give a shit about Bilbo Baggins and his bouncing clown act, or Shifty fucking Shirkin the shag pile rug suppliers. Fuck em all, just *move* the stupid queue along!

At *last,* a space becomes available, and the voice booms out through the Tanoy,

"Window number four please!"

The stupid, ugly, fat idiot of a woman – who's wearing a saggy blue rag for a top, hair un-brushed and her boobs half hanging out – she's next. She's the one who's supposed to go to the counter, but she's so preoccupied talking to her ugly fat mate about how cool she was downing a bottle of WKD with some sad night creature of a loser with no self-respect, in a losers bar only fourteen hours previously, she doesn't move to the window!!!

My head starts to fuzz, and a ringing starts in the ear. I walk round the outside of the queue, elbow the ill-fitting trash square in the face while calling her a *fucking idiot!* Then calmly move to the empty space at the window myself...to be served.

These impulsive psychotic delusions make me wonder to myself, am I just an impatient chap waiting in a queue, or am I a seriously unstable psychopath who's going to explode at any given moment? Or does everyone else think the same way as I do? Which would make everyone a psychopath. Or am I even a genius? I mean...you have to have the correct attitude towards these things haven't you? You know, so that things get done. It's the age-old question...'Is the glass half full, or half empty?' Which of course makes no sense to me whatsoever. I mean, who cares if it's half full or half fucking empty, JUST SO LONG AS THERE'S SOMETHING IN IT!

"Window number four please!" booms out again, the voice now in a 'losing patience' tone.

And would you believe it, she *still* hasn't finished talking drivel to her idiot friend. However, her friend gives her a nudge and this does the trick. *Now* she realises it's *her* turn. She makes a surprised gesture, as if she's somehow now important, almost like she's on stage, *then,* she slowly waddles her way to the counter. As if being an absolute scummy loser coming from trashville isn't enough, she proceeds in a very loud 'I want everyone to know my business' voice,

"How much to send this parcel to Spain?" and then looks around, as if for some sort of idiot approval.

Fucking Ebayers! Fucking wankers! I Fucking hate em!!!

Anyway, we all shuffle up a few inches, and the wheels are turning. *Hoo-fucking- rah!*

Chapter 3

Hard Man (Part 1)

She does her crap bit of sending the parcel off and leaves a space, which of course settles me a little because now there's one less obstruction to think about. The pen she used now dangles from the counter swinging lifelessly on its own momentum, waiting for the utilisation of more fingers with the cold or flu virus to pass on to someone else. The chain it hangs from... it's like a sink plug chain, why do they use them? Why can't they use a nice friendly luminous-glow orange fandango one, instead of the ones that always make you feel like you'd steal it if it *wasn't* chained down? Yeah right. As if I want a crap pen like that anyway...imbeciles!

"Window number one please!" booms out the voice again.

A bald man comes into view as he makes his way to the window. He's about six foot, eighteen stone, looks like a hard nut. (I know different) He wears a goatee beard, about forty-five years old with a leather waistcoat, jeans with steel toe-cap boots...polished. On his finger, he shows off the ring of the hell's angels, ha! who's he trying to kid?

I watch him closely as he asks for a book of first class stamps. He doesn't even take his wrap-round sunglasses off. Who in their right mind – if they want to see where they're going – wears sunglasses in a shop in the middle of winter? The thing is, I know this chap from the 'old skool.' Now then, is he really the hard nut he portrays himself to be, or is he just a self-conscious insecure paranoid wreck, warning people off with his menacing persona? The latter I think.

I punched him out once, that was before we kidnapped him and left him out in the woods tied to a tree...to think things over. Mind you, that was a while ago now, but looking at him, I remember that time as if it was this morning.

You see, he was talking to a couple of toke-the-weeders (People who smoke pot) in the local boozer, giving it all the hard-man bit about "knowing people, people who grow the stuff, and they ain't to be messed with." And how he could "get anything you want at any time." with this cocky hard core attitude.

Well good for you, I thought, as he stared menacingly at them through his paranoid eyes. But the two tokers seem to be impressed with his statement – they haven't been around long enough to know the difference between a monstrosity of a paranoid ego, and the real deal that they'll probably never meet, however, they lean in a little closer, as if there's now a deal going down.

My ears are so good, I can hear a baby crying for its mother from over two miles away; so I can definitely hear the street talking bullshit coming out of these idiots mouths, even though they are a good few feet away, and the fact that it's noisy in here. My ears are like satellite dishes, tuning in to any crapperhertz I want them to – a bonus of my condition, I suppose.

"Can you get us some white shark?" the rat-faced kid says almost excitedly, like if he gets some his mates will treat him like he's the don. He's only about nineteen-twenty years old, wearing a hoodie while trying to make his way through the ranks of drug respect and all that shite. 'Geezer' looks at him straight in the eye.

"You'd better not mess me around if I do." he says, giving him a hard stare. It's unbelievable that he's trying to act the hard man and gain respect from a couple of two bit kids if he does get *their* gear.

"No mate!" the other kid says. He's lanky, also sporting the street-life hoodie, and I think he's a ground worker or something, judging by his boots that are covered in mud and what-not.

"We wouldn't do that. If we order it, we pay."

My god! He's been watching too much TV as well ain't he?

So, 'Geezer' gets his phone out, and dials a number in front of them making the order. Lo and behold, ten minutes later... 'Bloke' walks in wearing a grin like a camel on ecstasy. 'Geezer' gets to his feet to greet him with a Mafioso hug and a pat on the back, you know, the way you see it on TV – the 'Cod-father' channel. A ridiculous handshake ensues that involves gripping each other's hands and playing funny finger games, as you would do at the age of about ten, and would've grown out of a long time ago.

So, 'Geezer' asks him what he wants to drink. "Fosters mate," 'Bloke' replies acting all the big boss, now that the dodgy crap-core handshakes are all done...and shown off to whoever's watching.

I almost fall about laughing at the sheer idiocy of this bloke. He wears a moody leather jacket, black jeans that don't fit properly, and white trainers that are too big for him, he looks totally ridiculous. 'Bloke' only deals because he's a lonely shit head with no communication skills, no friends, and wants to somehow gain some sort of recognition within the community of losers. If he didn't deal no one would want to know him, he's a slimy slug and only took up the practice so to make acquaintances, and be seen as cool – a total prick who's never going to change unless he gets a brain implant.

So anyway right, 'Geezer' introduces 'Bloke' to the tokers, and another kind of pussy handshake starts to ensue with the, 'I know the respect shake shit' and the 'we are the underworld' grins on their idiot faces.

'Bloke' and 'tokers' start chatting about who they know and what pubs they drink in, all the lightweight conversation that lasts for a few minutes before paranoia creeps in, because maybe they know something about each other that they shouldn't...(they may all be secret lightweights, who would sing from the highest mountain... once put under pressure, eh?)

However, 'Bloke' needs to do his homework (because you know how it is, he doesn't want to be treading on anyone's toes now, does he?) so, listening intently and nodding his head like a noddy boy does, he starts to get a picture. When he's got all the info he needs, and the way is clear, he pushes the sale a little deeper.

"Do you do speed or smarties?" (Amphetamines/Ecstasy) 'Bloke' asks, now knowing he could probably sell more than some cheap old weed to these tokers.

The tokers look at each other, and then back at Bloke. "Yeah" says rat face with his eyes now wider in anticipation. "Why, do you sell that too?"

"Yes mate." Bloke replies all jack the pancake. Prices start to emerge.

"Can you do us any posh?" (Cocaine) asks the ground worker a little tentatively.

"Can do." Bloke says, stringing his reply out with another grin, now realising he could be in for a new cardigan by the weekend.

They all start looking at each other, nodding slowly, as now they all know what's going on and where it's going down.

Bloke pipes up. "I'll go out to my motor and you follow me in a couple of minutes." he says, almost like an order.

"Cool," rat face says, giving him the nodding donkey look.

So there it is, five minutes into the deal, and all's going well for all involved. Bloke goes off and tokers follow after a couple of gulps of their golden liquid confidence. Now then, Geezer's now sitting on his own, and looking extremely paranoid. Four pints sitting on the table and only one person drinking – it doesn't take much to work it out, does it? (Either he's a prick and they've all fucked off and left him...or there's a deal going down) Anyway, Geezer's looking around to see if anyone's clocked what's going on. (which the whole pub probably has, but couldn't give a shit.)

I think to myself, *No one cares mate, only the managers, and they ain't here, so stop looking so menacingly paranoid and enjoy your pint! Prick!*

So, after five minutes or so the tokers come back in and sit down, trying to look like they've just been for a leak. Bloke isn't with them, his pint's still on the table.

"Cheers mate." says rat face contentedly sitting back in his chair, confidently sipping his pint.

"No worries." replies Geezer, feeling better now that he's not sitting on his own any more. "Is it okay?"

"Wicked!" rat face says. "It's going to stink the whole fucking house out!"

The table erupts with pretentious laughter as a relief of tension flows comfortably amongst them.

"Did you get anything else?" Geezer asks wonderingly.

"Yeah, got ten pills and a gram of posh." rat face replies being all jack-the-biscuit, inner pockets bulging.

"Cool" Geezer replies now thinking he's also got the 'Top banana dealer' status with a couple of two bit kids.

So, Geezer gets up and offers to buy them a drink, yeah? And I think, *What the fucks he up to now? Trying to make friends or something?* Anyway, they both accept.

"Fosters please mate" rat face says.

"For you too?" Geezer asks, looking at the ground worker.

"Please, mate." he replies.

Geezer goes off to the bar to order, right? Then it starts to look a bit odd. The tokers lean in to each other and start talking quietly, fast, as if there's a problem. Geezer returns to the table with three pints in his triangle shaped clasped hands, showing off his hard-core biker skull ring, and sets the drinks down.

"Cheers matey!" the tokers say almost in unison.

Then it goes into one of those uncomfortable silences for a minute or two as they take a few gulps of the new sweaty glass pints. Rat face pipes up, and looking at Geezer says,

"So, how well do you know this chap then?"

Geezer looks straight into rat face's eyes, as if he's said something wrong, almost angrily replying, "Long enough! why?"

Rat face quickly realising that geezer didn't like the question says,

"It's just that when we went to score at his motor, he said it wasn't his motor, it was yours, and we were wondering why has he come all this way down to sort us out with *your* gear, from *your* car ... when *you* could have sorted it yourself?"

"That bloke's a proper prat! And I don't know what he's on about! My car's not even here! But I can tell you what, he's going to get a punch from me when I see him next, I can tell ya!"

"Well, why don't you give him a bell now?" says rat face, looking a little confused.

"Nah! I'll do it later." Geezer exclaims as he looks away...thinking deeply.

What a complete and utter prick! Geezer's only just gone and employed a runner to flog his gear for him. The reason he's done this is so that no one suspects that Geezer's the real pusher, and then Bloke, who's supposed to be taking the heat off him, goes and shifts the real ownership back to Geezer, so now we all know that Geezer's the real pusher ... *WANKER!*

So, I'm outside on the phone to a very good long time friend of mine. "Hello, mate," I say as he answers my call. He knows who it is as my name would've been displayed on his phone.

"Haaaay! How are ya?" he replies.

"Yeah, I'm fine, thanks very much." I respectfully reply. We have a small chitchat about how each other's lives and families are, then on to why I phoned.

About twenty minutes later, we're sitting in his car – a very nice one may I add – with two of his friends who I haven't met before in the back, talking to each other in what sounds like polish. My friend introduces me to them, and in turn, we shake hands. (Normal shake) Both their hands are rough like manual labourers, and firm. I know these boys aren't for the soft touch that's for sure, which is good. I return to chatting with my friend for a while.

From where we're parked I can see the front door of the pub, like clockwork at this time of night out strolls Geezer. I wait until he's about two hundred yards away from the pub, and go to meet him on the pavement.

No words are spoken, a knee in the bollocks; he doubles up, an uppercut with my whole bodyweight behind it, and he's flat out on the pavement. Without showing pain in the fact that my hand feels like it's broken after that punch, my friend and his two accomplices join me as we pick the heavy lump up.

Puffing and panting we struggle to get the unconscious lump on to the back seat of the car. My friend's friends sit either side of him. We put duck tape over his mouth, around his wrists and legs, and then put a stinking black cloth bag over his head. He's now sitting there totally unable to move or talk, which is good, because no one wants to hear any more shit coming from this pricks mouth tonight – and that's a fact.

My friend puts his foot on the accelerator, roaring the engine effortlessly to glide the car up the road with a thrust that pushes me back into the arm-chair-type grey leather seat. Much more effortlessly than the last few minutes have been, that's the truth; this car's an automatic – smooth and fast.

***

"Window number four please." rings out.

I look at him. He's aged, but still the wannabe hard-man prick I've always known.

The queue shuffles along a little, again, the wheels are turning. Thank fuck for that, because I'm starting to need a piss! And if I can't hold it...I'll do it where I am.

Anyway before I finish this story about Twat-bollocks Geezer, I've just noticed – while trying to look at the door that exits this area into a gardening department – out of the corner off my eye, I can see a chap I haven't seen for a long time, a different kind of breed altogether. He's looking at the seeds and flowers section, checking prices on gardening tools and all that, which is a little strange for this one, (Unless he's going to a funeral) as this chap's an absolute and total nutter if *ever* I've known one. He's a proper weird one, with no fear, the worst type, especially after a couple of beers when someone pisses him off. He reminds me of someone I knew a long time ago, someone who I held a great deal of respect for.

He stands around five feet six inches, forty-odd years old, bald, stocky, wearing a pair of black farer trousers that went out of fashion thirty years ago. He wears a pin through collared shirt, covered by a three-quarter length mohair coat with a red silk triangle piece peeking from the left breast pocket and well polished tan brown loafers for shoes. He's an old-time rude boy, from the times of the specials – Ghost Town and all that. However out of date he looks, he still looks smart, presentable and oozing with confidence...and of course, he still carries the cheeky-chappy grin.

He disappeared for years when he was about twenty-one years old, went on walkabout by all accounts. When he turned up a good few years later, I overheard a conversation about him down the local boozer. Apparently he'd gone a bit loony, talking about aliens and stuff, how the government was covering up all evidence of the ET's and how the they were already in touch with them. You know, stuff that doesn't do well for light pub conversation, but does do well to get a reputation for being a little weird to say the least.

Some say he'd been out of the country and mixing with the wrong people, doing drugs and losing his head. I don't think they knew what they were talking about, considering I overheard another story about him which made a lot more sense, that came from a reputable source, and was a shed-load more believable than the other rubbishy small talk you hear from the small-village types.

It was when he was in Thailand. Yep, I remember this one well, it's not the sort of thing you forget. By the time I heard this story, he'd solidified himself a nickname: 'the nutter' (as well as other names) – and by all accounts he'd just spent nine years in the forces, six in the regular, and three in the specials. This is what I heard...

Chapter 4

The Nutter Rides Out

Day 1

His small black raggedy rucksack didn't house much. Tightly rolled, he stuffed it with only a pair of shorts, T-shirt, flip-flops, toothbrush, toothpaste and a towel. The passport travellers' cheques and five thousand baht in notes went into the money belt that fitted snugly round his ailing six pack, now resembling more of a nine-gallon barrel.

His mate gave him a lift to Heathrow airport as he was flying with Emirates, meaning all food, drink and everything else was in on the fare which was great, because if there's one thing the nutter had gotten very used to... it was the booze.

So there he was on the plane. A 747, a big bird. He had footrests (adjustable) a good seat by the window (adjustable) and a TV with thirty channels (four being film) all nicely built into the headrest of the seat in front – oh ... and armrests. The plane was bright with a clean holiday smell, which carried a buzz from the people on board for destinations unknown to him.

Pleasantly presented with a three-course meal and booze menu from the pocket in the back of the seat in front, he lays them out on the now fully extended plastic table, almost like it's a million pound deal, careful to position it dimensionally, in line with the sides of the table, while pondering with delight. As much as food and drink to him has always just been fuel, he still now and again enjoys the choices presented.

The blue and white suede size-eight puma trainers play with the swivelling foot rests, as the elbows and hands find comfort on the cool steel of the solid arm rests. The sexy attendants who always look so fantastic in their uniforms organize things around him. They pack hand luggage into the overhead compartments, stretching themselves over the seated area, almost deliberately to give off the fantastic horny sight of their splendid tightness around the bust area...more than enough for the nutter's imagination to cope with, he's got a buzz going on like he's just set himself up for a dead-cert in his youth, half anticipation, half apprehension.

Lifting his arse off the seat slightly while digging around in the front of his Levis 501 red-tab pockets, he locates the valium a mate gave him the day before. Gently feeling them with his fingertips recognising their shapes, gives confirmation of a good kip, and that, mixed with thoughts of Thai ladies prompts a broad grin. When he's ready, they'll go down loosely with a large gulp of Australian red, then off to the land of nod for a few hours with not too much jet lag after the journey, just the way he likes it.

Thirty thousand feet in the air, and with a fourteen-hour flight ahead of him, he starts on the booze, slowly at first, only half bottles of red at a time.

By the time he arrives at Bangkok airport, he's unshaven, drunk, and stinks worse than a pack of skunks with the breath of an alcoholic's kidney. He only just remembers stopping off at Bahrain in a drunken half drugged up state while changing flights to Bangkok. That in itself was a miracle. Here, he also managed to change from his English weather-worn clothes, to hot Thai-sunshine clothes, which he had previously tightly stuffed in his bag. However, washing and shaving with a quick spruce up wasn't on the agenda. With no baggage, only the rucksack on his back, baggage collection didn't apply.

The brightly lit Bangkok arrivals lounge sported the usual airport comings and goings, a din in the air mixed with Thai language booming through the public announcements speakers making the whole scenario a little surreal. The daytime sunshine separating false lighting from real flooded in from below the exit sign, so as to guide this stinking drunk to the silver automatic exit doors, and out to the haze of a Thai morning heat.

It hits him like a brick wall. He's sure he's just walked from the fridge into a fire. His clothes immediately stick to him like cling-film around a sandwich. Beads of sweat ooze from pores all over his quickly clammy body.

"Hello, taxi?"

Turning round, while still trying to come to terms with the climate and looking over his left shoulder, an English-speaking Thai man's shouting at him to get in his cab. A welcoming feeling flows over him by way of this person beckoning him into the clean blue-and-yellow vehicle. Knowing he'll be needing a ride at one stage or another, rather than taking a lucky guess with the other Thai transport, he agrees to the offer, and makes his way over.

The Thai, being the perfect host, goes to take his small rucksack, but the nutter mumbles, "No, it's okay mate, I'll keep it with me," as he climbs through the open door of the car settling into the cool comfy clean leather seat tucking the rucksack down into the foot well. *Nice and cool, lucky these baby's are air con,* he thinks as the sweat immediately begins to dry on his forehead.

The cab smells like oranges, well organised with the cabby's identification card displayed for all passengers to see. This is their livelihood, so keeping it clean, tidy, and all up-to-date is a must. The happy cabby climbs in pulling the door.

"Where you go?" he asks with a genuine smile on the darkly tanned smooth skinned face. Looking at the drunken bum, he's knows he's in for a good fare.

"Er ... hotel please mate"

"Oh, okay, hote' where?" he says almost sarcastically.

"Hotel down koa-sang-roe?" says nutter, knowing the cabby's heard this a million times before from all English-speaking single travellers, so he'll know to take him straight there, no messing about ... won't he?

"Okay." says the Thai setting the trip meter to twenty baht.

The ride's comfortable and swift. The cabby acts just like any other taxi man from London, or Sussex – just not saying too much, probably because as it turns out his English is very limited. And as the nutter doesn't speak Thai, there's not really much to talk about; they could talk about the weather if they understood each other ... but then again, there's not much change in the Thai weather either, except for the odd downpour. So he just watches the landscape as it flows by, and in all honesty, as much as he knows he's in Thailand, it still doesn't sink in properly. The alcohol mixed with other narcotics still runs through his veins. Not knowing what to expect from the country, he sits back enjoying the ride.

"You wan foo?" the Thai asks, without taking his eyes off the bright-grey tarmac road.

"Eh? Oh food. Yeah okay, but first hotel." he replies wanting to get settled in, cleaned up and organised before any shenanigans take place, which he knows there will be within the next day or so.

"Okay." says cabby, with a smile... and a twinkle in his eye.

After twenty minutes or so, the cab pulls up at a small two-level building resembling a hotel. The Thai gets out slowly walking around the car wearing a cheeky grin, as he nods towards the front doors of building, then opens the car door for the nutter to get out.

"Is this the hotel?" he asks looking at the cabby a little concerned, hoping it's not; because it doesn't look that big, and to be fair, it's in the middle of nowhere. In fact ...*Where are we?* he thinks as his guard begins to rise.

"Yes, yes, yes, you come?" says the cabby trying to instil a bit of confidence, and smiling even broader, gesturing the nutter towards the main entrance by way of his hands, slowly back-palming the path, like it's the yellow brick road or something.

The nutter's been in a lot more precarious situations than this, and by all accounts he *can* look after himself; he's pretty up on the unarmed combat, and if need be he's quick enough on his heels too. So, he decides to go with the flow, if push comes to shove, he'll punch the cabby on the nose, then nick his car.

Nutter grabs his rucksack following the Thai up the well-presented marble path, which leads to the front of some doors, in the middle of nowhere. Still feeling this somehow isn't quite right, really, he has no choice but to relax into the situation, thinking, *Well...In for a penny, in for a pound.*

The clean bright aluminium doors open outwards, almost like they're automatic. There's a well-dressed thickset Thai man inside. His suit's a grey-silver tone and looks expensive. Recognising the handmade suit as cashmere, this somehow eases the nutter's mind. If the Thai's wearing a good suit, especially in the six-thousand-degree heat, then at least he takes pride in how he's dressed. *So there's nothing wrong with having a look ... is there?* he thinks with confidence building.

The suit welcomes him through the doors. Well, what greets the nutter (whose name is Mack) is far from a hotel. In fact, if all hotels were like this one...then busy would be their middle name. Looking around, Mack realises he may well have just struck gold...

Chapter 5

A Golden Pitstop

Jeeezaaaas! I wasn't prepared for this so soon! his mind shouts. Taking a quick glance around the large room, it's cool, not like the fierce heat from outside, and at the far end of the room is a small bar advertising Heineken, Chang, and a couple of other alcoholic drinks. *Well, at least they've got a bar.* he thinks again, trying to focus on exactly what they have to sell, while instinctively moving towards it. The feeling of an inner smile is becoming apparent, in fact, after looking around, he's beginning to feel properly at home.

In the middle of the clean and well-decorated room with white plaster moulding and quality patterns on the ceiling and walls, is an oval-shaped comfy-looking red leather sofa. This completely encircles a large pillar, which nestles nicely on a blue-carpeted floor. To the left is what looks like a small ten-by-ten parquet dance floor. Of course, as if it's the norm, it boasts a shiny silver pole in the middle, running from floor to ceiling.

To the right, there's a kind of two-level seating area, which runs the whole width of the wall, draped in about twenty feet or so of what looks like the texture and colour of red silk.

Sitting on this silky showpiece...are about twenty of the fittest, most gorgeous-looking Thai girls he's ever seen in his life. (Except in porn mags and vids) Mack's eyes nearly pop out of his head with approval. They're all wearing white hotel towelling robes, glowing with brown shiny skin, oozing with sex appeal. A glass wall separates the area from where Mack stands, allowing a view of a line of sexy goddesses! *YIPPEE! It's a fucking whore house! Wow! The cabby must have known what I wanted before I did...nice.*

The suited Thai says, "Sit, sit, sit." with a welcoming smile as he gestures Mack towards the sofa. Mack takes a pew, getting comfortable while gawping in awe at what he can help himself too. He's been to whore-houses many times before, but never one so organised, regulated and clean – with all the women being so out-of-this-world stunning.

"Choose!" the suit says, casting a long arm along the ladies behind the screen.

Mack says slowly aloud with his eyes wide, "Choose then, eh?"

"Yes." he says in a quiet voice, with a smile, looking again at the ladies.

Ohhhh kay, Mack thinks as he eyes up the goods.

Slowly, casting his now sex-hungry eyes over the goddesses of passion, he stops at one, then moves to another. They're all looking at him...some look stern, others look sheepish. He knows he's now shopping for a piece of the real action, and wants his purchase to be just right.

All of them are the same colour, tanned like the colour of someone who's sat on the beach for a couple of weeks. Not burnt, but tanned. Their make-up is extremely well done – some are over the top, others with hardly any. He wonders why it is that at home make-up doesn't look so good on a tanned person, but on some of these ladies, it looks perfect.

Now they're all looking at Mack with smiles, slowly leaning their heads from left to right as if asking the question of whether he fancies them or not. Mack thinks they all fancy him.

One in particular stands out from the rest; she has a great pair of tits, and a look of really wanting him to pick her. His eyes try to see more of her behind the white gown. Noticing his interest she lets the gown slip slightly from her shoulders, giving just a peek at the top of the smooth bare flesh of the warm breasts. They're not only big, but firm – nipples pointing outwards, now visible through her robe which speaks volumes. She obviously looks after her well-kept, long, black, permed hair. A nice – not cheeky or dirty, but nice – smile too. Well, that does it for him.

"Okay." he says, making his mind up, pointing at her.

With that, the suit gets up and swiftly moves to speak with another Thai lady who's not in robes. This one wears a stark grey suit. She's a lot older and has the look and grace of a foreign headmistress about her. Swiftly she goes behind the screen saying something to the broad who Mack's pointed out.

The broad follows the mistress out from behind the screen and gracefully walks over to Mack. Stopping in front of him, she puts her hands together with a smile and a bow. The headmistress approaches Mack; bluntly, and with no emotion she barks, "1,500 baht!" while holding her hand out.

Mack doesn't care about her abruptness and jealousy. By this stage, he's mesmerized by the Thai broad. Groping around in his money belt he hands over two thousand-baht notes to the stern lady, while gazing over the broad's figure knowing the body under the robes will be blissfully his in a very short while, and not the lady taking the money – which doesn't make her look back in anger in any way shape or form.

From behind the bar she lays his change on the wooden bar top, a five-hundred-baht note with a stern bow, but no smile. Mack's starting to sober up by this time and needs some more of the juice to limber him up.

If the time is now his, he can do as he pleases with his new date; so, he asks if she'd like a drink so he can have one too. He purchases a Heineken, and a soft drink for her, and contentedly sits at the bar. After a few gulps of the cold lager, it all starts to feel a little uncomfortable...what with him being the only punter in there, twenty-odd Thai ladies sitting to his right, unemployed by all accounts. Then there's the suit behind him, standing with his arms crossed, the stern Thai lady, glaring at him from behind the bar. The the non-existent conversation with the broad directly to his right, who's sipping uncomfortably away at her lemonade, she indicates that getting straight down to business would be a good manoeuvre; Mack nods his head in agreement.

Beckoning Mack to follow her, she leads the way leaving the uncomfortable atmosphere of the empty of punters bar and lounge well behind. The rich-looking shop window and blue pile carpets lead to a stone-floored corridor. The glitz turns to seedy as the unpainted, stone, thin surrounding corridor lead to some steps. Up the stone steps and round a corner where another broad sits on the stone floor doing her make-up, shuffling over to make room for them to pass.

His purchase leads him into a bathroom, once inside the broad wastes no time in locking the door and turning the taps on to run a hot bubbly bath. She turns and reaches to grasp the bottom of his T-shirt, then moves to his belt. *Whahay!* he thinks as the deal begins.

Getting the gist of things, he undresses himself as the broad disrobes, both of them standing there with Mack not knowing if this is bath sex or what?. She gently ushers him into the bath, and starts to wash him all over. Mack's loving it, a hot bath, and being pampered by a beautiful Thai lady ... what could be better?

With his stinking body fully relieved of its London to Thailand journey and smelling good, she helps him out and then towels him down. Mack's enjoyed it so much he wants to repay the complement and says, "You, now."

She looks at him a little confused, "Me?"

"Yeah, you," he says wanting to return the pleasantries.

She shrugs her shoulders, a little unsure; with her eyes dubiously on him, she gets into the tub. Mack gets the soap and sponge and starts to wash her as if he's doing the daily washing up.

She's now getting into it too, realising this chap's a harmless nutter she looks at him with a playful smile, letting out a happy giggle.

Mack gets on with the job in hand while whistling contentedly away and thinking, *That's fine, let's all get clean and fresh.*

With the bathroom episode complete, they're now clean dry and ready. She leads him to another room where drapes hang over the windows. It does now in fact resemble a hotel room. Taking her towel off exposing her perfectly shaped figure, she gestures for him to put his stuff down on the dresser, and then get comfortable on the white-sheeted clinical bed.

For the first time Mack feels a little uncomfortable. He's now going to be more than a hand's length from his money belt, which carries his passport, money and other necessary paperwork. However, he calculates that she wouldn't have time to grab his belt, unlock the door, and make an exit before he stopped her. So he lies on the bed, face down, and gets comfortable with one eye on his belt, which is lying well in view on the dressing table. She puts a small white towel over his bottom, leaving him less exposed.

Locking the door, she turns and smiles at him. She takes a small bottle of oil from the dresser, warms it up in her hands, and expertly starts massaging that warm oil into his shoulders. Scent from her hands now fills the room. *Lavender ... how relaxing.*

Mack's muscles get a good work out by the expert foreign hands, relaxing him massively. Gently she gets on the bed, sitting on the back of his legs, moving them apart to accommodate her warm firm round bottom. More oil into his muscles, into his back, and down to his waist. She moves the towel over the lower part of his bottom and massages the tops of his cheeks, all of his cheeks and down the backs of his legs, which gives Mack a great sense of relaxation and, inevitably, a hard on.

The broad gets off, releasing the blood to flow to its full circulation. Of course, this does immediate wonders for the proverbials, giving to an instant rush of blood, which makes lying on his front a little uncomfortable.

He's feeling exactly as the broad has expertly directed. As he turns over onto his back, the obviousness of her actions springs into view. The broad lets out a happy giggle smiling contentedly at Mack, as she eyes up what her work so far has achieved.

Standing by the bed, she then straddles him, sitting just below his midsection on the thighs. Slowly, she leans over which gives a fantastic view of her large, very firm, most suck-able tits. Occasionally she strokes her warm large brown erect nipples on his chest, as the momentous movements make this happen. She carries on the massage on his shoulders, chest, arms, and then moves her way down onto the midsection ... the tender area.

The broad, with a flick of her head, throws her long black permed hair up and forwards over her head, and onto his chest, making the stomach muscles spasm slightly with the slight whipping sensation this has created. Dragging her face and hair down his torso, the warmth of her mouth engulfs his piece making the buttocks tense, making the last drops of blood fill his cock to the full. She's now giving head. His hands instinctively go to the back of *her* head, to feel its reality, to clarify the reality of the sensation he feels. Mack just hopes he's not having a dream whilst on the plane over.

On her way up he notices that somehow, and without him realising it, she's managed to get a Durex on him. *Clever*, he thinks loving the attention to detail that she's giving. Having aroused his member to a piece resembling red and blue steel, she can now move on to earn the money properly.

Manoeuvring herself over it, with her knees either side of Mack, she slowly positions herself. A slight wiggle of the hips and a slow downwards motion, the pussy engulfs his member going all the way down, only skin, pubic hair, and a little body fat to separate their slightly quivering pubic bones, holding their positions for a second or two. They breathe out in sequence, a contented sigh, staying motionless for a few seconds to take in the warmth – she, from being filled to the max by girth and length; he, by way of the moist soft snug warmth that only comes with this exercise.

Starting slowly at first, moving into faster and more rhythmic motions, she's rocking her body back and forth, arching her back, sitting as deep on him as possible. The firm tits give Mack the view of a lifetime. The whole date's going fantastically for them both. Mack's groping her perfect breasts, cupping them while feeling their smooth firmness, squeezing her nipples gently. Her eyes are closed and from what he can see from her expression, she is fully concentrated. Mack's hands firmly feel down the side of her concave figure, finishing by gripping her perfect thighs. Her heels are tucked tightly under her legs, gripping Mack's sides like a clamp. She's upping her movements to a trot, like she's trotting a seventeen-hand horse on a summers afternoon. He's got hold of her hips, getting into the stride and helping her all the way.

A few minutes into the momentous rhythm, Mack can feel things starting to stir deep inside his loins. He wants to get a little more control of the situation, holding off for as long as he can, but if he's going to bolt, he wants to do it properly. Not wanting this smooth, rhythmic fuck any more, he wants to get into her from behind. He wants more – absolute full penetration with more room for pumping, more manoeuvrability for giving the full length to this fantastic broad, to take it away from her, then to give it back ... with a slam.

He motions for her to get off. They shift round. She's seemingly a little pissed off with him breaking her concentration. Again, he gets a whole view of her beautifully tanned smooth perfectly shaped figure. "Fantastic!" he mumbles, shaking his head slowly in total and absolute approving lust.

As if she knows what he wants, she gets into position on all fours, arching her back while pushing up the honey pot so he can't miss. He doesn't. Mack slides his piece as far into her pussy and as deep as he can, making their bodies as one again. The broad groans.

Holding in her as deep as he can, a slow full-length withdrawal makes for the full feeling of her warm lubricated tightness as he watches the bulb of his member slowly come into view. Holding the bulb just at the entrance of her folds, he slides it back in, repeating the process, getting faster and faster until the rhythm is almost frantic. He's fucking her like there's no tomorrow. Legs bent, knees just above her perfectly smooth round bottom, hands on her shoulders, he feels like a crazed animal, totally going for it. No romance whatsoever, just pure animal instincts letting loose on the one thing we all have when finding this state of mind – hard sweaty sex.

A few hard pumping sweaty minutes go quickly as he comes, grunting like a knackered horse, all the senses gone, only pure ecstasy flowing through the body in a uncontrolled wave as his soul leaves his body for that split second, connecting with all spiritual surroundings, and back again. Mack collapses onto her back, his body in spasms like a finger in a plug socket. The spasms slow as the last of the body's life fluids are caught by the man made glove.

Breathing heavily and slightly dribbling, he rests his now heaving chest, head and arms on her still pumping sweaty back. She's now on her own, looking for that soul release. Mack doesn't care for her pleasure but realises she's nearly there, so lets her get on with it. He holds his position and grabs her saddle, holding the middle finger in the crease of the hips to hold her in deep as she keeps humping his member. Her back jerks upwards as her head contorts into her chest, arms and hands, now holding him exactly where he is, balancing on her forehead. She slumps forward, half onto her side, shaking with eyes held tightly shut and breathing heavily. Mack knows she's just orgasmed. A quick thought that maybe she should be paying him flashes through his mind.

With the relief of all that's just taken place, he laughs out loud. She opens her eyes, gathering her senses. With her body starting to relax, she starts to quietly laugh with him. He falls sideways off her as a large long breath escapes his lungs. They lie there like a married couple ... both needing their bodies to find the energy to get themselves together, or have a smoke.

The energy comes back for the broad, who slowly, and seemingly a little embarrassed, makes the moves to get herself together as she avoids his eyes. Mack follows her actions with a knowing grin. The warming glow that's engulfed them both is now making the feeling of this being a monetary transaction disappear.

Before going downstairs, she hands Mack a card with her name and number, after writing her mobile number down too. Looking at him straight in the eyes, she tells him she'll travel anywhere in Bangkok to meet him, and he can have her all night for the price he's just paid here. Working out that he's just paid £20, Mack thinks this is a good deal and tucks the card into his money belt with a smile. Knowing how the last forty-five minutes has been, this card is priceless.

Back downstairs, where the other Thai lady is, he thanks everyone around for his unexpected delight and is shown out by the suit, who in return says thank you and good-bye, giving Mack a typical English thumbs up.

Outside from the fridge and into the fire, the taxi man's still there, which is a pleasant surprise for Mack; he's been at least forty-five minutes and isn't used to cabbies waiting for more than five minutes. Mack now feels like he knows the cabby a little. The cabby opens the door and says with a smile, "Foo now eh?"

Mack gets in with a relaxed and refreshed expression. The twinkle in Mack's eye tells the cabby he'd be more than happy with some food now.

"You li' sea foo'?" the taxi man asks,

"Yeah, I li' see foo'," Mack replies cockily mimicking his accent, and off they go again.

Mack's happy with his trip so far. He's been in Thailand for not much over an hour or so, and already he's had a bath, got laid by one of the most beautiful women on the planet, and now he's on his way to a restaurant, and he still doesn't even know quite where he is...excellent.

Chapter 6

The fish market

Slowly the cab pulls into what only can only be described as a makeshift, dusty falling-down fish market. It looks closed; there's only a few stalls left open with malodorous fish heads on display as large bluebottles buzz around, eating and regurgitate over them. The fish heads glazed eyeballs and dry open mouths greet him like a late arrival. There's none of the expected hustle and bustle of a market, only Thai stallholders packing things away as they talk quietly to each other about the disappointing sales of the day.

Cabby gets out opening the door for Mack, who slowly gets out, dubiously casting his eyes around the seemingly non-touristy venue.

"Okay, we eat," the cabby says like 'this is where all the posh people eat' – Mack thinks it's more like a place where he would bring unsuspecting drunks straight from the whore house, for whatever's left over. Indeed, being stitched up is in the air now.

The overwhelming smell of raw fresh fish overcomes any other possible smell in the vicinity, magnified by the second in the quickly heating day. It's more than enough to put Mack off his appetite; however, not to offend his new friend he says nothing, putting his trust in the cabby, and again he manages to sooth his inhibitions going with the flow.

A large fish tank sprawls down one whole side of a whitewashed wall, which just so happens to be the only clean wall in the area. Inside, there have to be fifty or so king prawns, walking around on their wispy legs, small black eyes looking around for a release from the confining surroundings, and a way back to the sea, with no cage of glass to hold them till death.

"You li' praw'?" the cabby asks.

Slowly Mack replies, "Yeah, okay," now realising that unless he wants manky fish heads for brunch, these babies will do just fine.

The cabby leads the way through a door into a well-furnished and adequately comfy restaurant, which of course is bang next door to the fish market and prawn tank. A waitress quickly makes her way over once she's been noisily summoned by the cabby. With a lovely smile, she gracefully shows Mack to a well-presented table that boasts a clean white table cloth, all laid with silver cutlery. The other tables are just tables with cloths over them, almost like Mack had missed the party by an hour or so. Or was he expected?

In all honesty, the restaurant looks a little expensive for his tastes. However, the cabby's looked after him so far, so ... *come on, let's have it!*

Mack waits in the comfy red-padded chair while looking around and thinking, *Okay, I've ordered prawns, but what's coming with it? Naked waitresses?....* he can only hope.

No more than ten minutes later, his questions are answered. The well-dressed waitress comes over with a sizzling bowl of prawns, pink and smelling like the Ritz hotel's kitchen on a top-class seafood night. The aroma of garlic and freshly cooked prawns is a far cry from the stench outside, again he realises that he's being looked after.

And that's it ... just a huge bowl of sizzling prawns, and a couple of dips. Mack's used to having some chow mien or something of that description to go with it, so...he sits there waiting for the other dishes to arrive.

The smiling waitress stands there, patiently waiting, smiling even more broadly every time Mack looks at her as he waits for the next dish.

After a couple of minutes of them all looking at the prawns, and at each other, Mack starts to feel a little uncomfortable, like he's doing something wrong. The Thai waitress says something to Mack in Thai, but of course he has no idea what she's going on about, so he just smiles back at her. He's starting to think that the prawns will get cold by the time the other dish arrives. Mack looks at the cabby with a 'help me' look as he realises that maybe another plate isn't coming. The cabby gestures for him to eat but Mack still doesn't go for it. Now the cabby looks confused.

The cabby and waitress have a quick chat. The cabby picks up a prawn and holds it out to Mack, Mack takes it, now knowing he's got to do something with it, starts to clumsily pull it about. With that, the head comes off with a small puff of steam. Then he pulls at the tail, but this doesn't work, the tail bits seem to half come off, and Mack's got it all over his now greasy hands while the prawn looks like it's been through a masher.

The waitress looks at the cabby, the cabby looks at the waitress, the waitress giggles a little, putting her hand over her mouth. The cabby looks disappointingly at Mack as if to say, "We've got a right one here." She giggles again, realising Mack has no idea what he's doing. She picks one up and holds it out to him, then shows her skill as her delicate fingers masterfully hold the prawn out for Mack to see as she peels it in a split second, then gently feeds it to him, wearing a grin but holding her composure, not like the broad from earlier at all. However, this one's probably only earning a fraction of what the broad earns, and yet this one seems so much more attractive.

Mack picks a prawn up, holding it over the plate. He nearly gets it right this time, with only a few legs left on. She then gestures towards the small bowls of dips. He tries the red dip. *Wow! Absolutely delicious!* he says to himself, tasting the sweet chilli and prawn together as the delicate flavours fill his glands and the prawns melt in his mouth, taking away all embarrassment.

His phone bleeps loudly, reminding him of the reason he is in Thailand. With greasy fingers he dives for the rucksack fumbling around for the phone. It's a message; his mobile provider lets him know he can now receive a signal and roaming is now in place. *Good,* he thinks. Now he can phone his contact for the Turk back home, and get this deal moving. *Thirty-three thousand pounds for a couple of week's work ...not bad,* he thinks. *Let's get it in the bank!"*

Mack can't eat all the prawns, there's far too many. He gestures over the table for the cabby to help him out, so as not to waste such a delicious plate of food, which the cabby happily does as he receives the plate it slides across the table. Shrugging his shoulders, he gets stuck into the now discarded prawns.

The greasy empty plate sits in front of the cabby as Mack finishes the bottle of beer. He's got a full stomach and a feeling of extreme contentment, time to go. Leaving the cleaners to finish their job around him, and paying with a large tip for the waitress, they head back to the now familiar cab.

The cabby's now sold everything he can to Mack, except for a suit and some precious stones that aren't worth a light once home. Now it's time to get Mack to a hotel.

"How mu' you pay fo' hotel fo' one nigh'?" the cabby asks.

Knowing the currency he replies, "Three hundred and fifty Baht."

"Okay," the cabby replies, now wanting to help the foreigner to a good hotel for a good price.

Mack looks out of the window as they travel towards the hotel. He sees the surroundings are now turning from the suburbs to urban areas – very urban indeed. In fact, there's no spare space in the city to swing a cat, and if there was, then the beggar that shuffles around on his bottom with his seriously deformed body would make a house out of cardboard in that space; in fact, he already has.

Bright lights, big bright neon signs, noisy police whistles, shops, motor bikes with riders on with no helmets, more cabs than Paddington station and huge towering buildings surrounded by a rush of people. Mack's in the thick of it – and to be honest, he's loving it.

The cabby pulls down a busy street where tuk-tuks, foot massages, suit shops, and many other ongoing businesses are buzzing around; they offer services and products in exchange for baht to feed their families. The cab slows to the kerb stopping outside a well-lit hotel entrance.

Breathing in the Bangkok ambiance, it's hot, sticky with the smell of sewage. Following the cabby through the front doors and into a well presented reception area, the cabby talks to the well-dressed grey/black uniformed receptionist, who in turn smiles at Mack, saying,

"Sawadeeka." Like all the Thais he's met so far, she gracefully bows her shiny tanned face down with her hands together.

Mack replies with a blunt "Hello."

Checking in with the receptionist, the cabby patiently waits close by to be paid. Mack hands in his passport, and 750 baht (three nights' stay.) Turning to the cabby and wincing he asks,

"How much?"

The cabby asks for one hundred baht. Mack pays him happily, knowing he hasn't been ripped off. Thinking back, he remembers the suit at the brothel giving the cabby something as they were leaving, pieces of paper with a red emblem on them, which looked like the ESSO petrol logo. Maybe they were part of the fare? The receptionist hands him a pair of keys, one for the main doors and one for his room, number ten.

Following the directions she gave him; in the lift, third floor, and around the red-carpeted corridor. The room number greets him. Unlocking the solid dark-brown wooden door, he's pleasantly surprised; for the price, it's got Sky TV, a king-size bed, air con, a full ceramic with chrome fittings shower area, a wardrobe, a phone with a menu sitting up straight next to the bedside table lamps, a mahogany desk and chair with writing paper on a green leather mat. The red carpet has no stains and the walls are clean. The whole room smells clean and fresh; not bad for about ten quid a night. The cabby has done well.

Flicking the inside of the brass door-catch to the lock position and checking the window for its view, it isn't clever, the workings of the air-conditioning unit is noisy and a view of a brick wall that leads to a thin alleyway twenty feet below is it.

Checking out the channels on the TV for a while, his eyes get heavy as going over his future plans come to the forefront of his mind. He needs a map. After all that's happened in the first couple of hours of being in Thailand, he still doesn't even know where he is, or in fact how he got there; but getting his bearings is important. Slowly, he drifts into the realms of semi-consciousness. With a smile, he remembers the personal service he gave the broad earlier, while of course thoroughly servicing himself. *Lucky cow.*

***

Someone's just bumped into me from behind, fucking nice one! looking around for a culprit, I can't see one. Any way, now my train of thought's gone, I'll carry on with Mack in a bit. This dickhead geezer's nearly done at the counter, which has reminded me off how his little escapade ended.

Chapter 7

Hard Man (part 2) Irony

About fifteen minutes into the ride which I'm thoroughly enjoying, I can hear Geezer groaning as he starts to come round. He's not struggling or kicking up a fuss, probably just confused as to where he is and what's going on, which is cool, as panic never did anyone any good.

Another fifteen minutes later my friend pulls into a large car park which is surrounded by an extremely dark and dense forest, slowly bringing the car to a halt. We all look at each other in the darkness, as if to say, "Here we are then, let's do it."

Looking at Geezer, he's in a very submissive and sorry state, sitting there, bound gagged and with a bag over his head like an SAS captive. My friend gets out, goes round to the boot and noisily gets out a sack trolley clanking it down on the car park surface then bringing it round to the car door. There's a push from inside the car as we roughly manhandle Geezer onto his new transport, feet first and bolt upright. The sack trolley's only just coping with geezer's weight as he's wheeled down the bumpy track. *It's lucky we're going downhill and not up, as this fat fucker would be a proper struggle.* The fresh, cool essence of pine smells strong in the cold thick air; which is funny, because it's the same scent as my friend's air freshener in his car. Or has the residue of the freshener stuck to my nasal hairs? Well whatever it is, it's nice, anyway.

As we wheel the trolley with Geezer on it over a load of rough ground, a wheel jams into a small crevice, jolting the trolley forward and tipping him onto the ground, landing him on his side with a heavy thump that almost echoes.

I can feel our obtrusive night time escapades are not being welcomed by the denseness of this secluded beauty spot. The atmosphere around seems to want us to leave it in peace and stop being so melodramatic; however, drama is the only thing it seems this idiot of a dealer understands, so the forest will just have to accommodate us, just this once.

I look at my friend who I can just see in the dim night light. He looks at me as if I'm going to say something, so I do.

"Fuck it! We'll tie him up here," I say in a can't-be-bothered tone.

"Fair enough," my friend replies, also in a not-bothered tone.

He lays the trolley down and we get Geezer to his feet. I reach for my knife and cut the tape around his legs so he can now walk unaided. As if we were the police escorting a criminal, we take him off the track and into the denseness of the forest area. The dead twigs and forest foliage are spongy with a springy feel underfoot. Finding a tree that accommodates this prick isn't difficult; there are thousands of them, possibly millions, all now looking angrily back at us.

Turning him around, with his back to the rough bark, he's held tightly to it by my new friends as I take the duct tape out of my pocket. We wrap the tape round him and the tree until he starts to look like a grey cocoon. His head hangs down on his chest in dejection, as his heavy lump of a body is held firmly taut against the cold rough exterior of the tree bark. We all stand there for a few minutes just looking at him, not saying a word.

I'm wondering what he's thinking, so I ask, "What are you thinking then mate?"

The squeaking noise that comes from inside his taped-up mouth says it all. My friends suggest that they'll meet me back at the car in a while as it's now a *personal* deal.

Moving my face to Geezers, nearly pressing it up to his, I take the bag off his head and the tape off his mouth. He doesn't murmur a word. I can just see the expression on his face in the dim light. He wears the look of a question – a 'what are you going to do to me? Question. *So now it's time.*

"Now then mate," I start, "How did that little jerk of a runner get the keys to your car?"

I look at him, my head tilted and my eyes wide, waiting for an explanation that doesn't come. "It's not that I want to tell you how to do your business, but please sort out that dick-head looking prick you've stupidly employed and let's not have an episode like that again. If – at the end of the day – you and your car are being tagged, then when he goes to your car, the police will do an ownership check . Then, of course, my name and address pops up, and I get busted, don't I? That's *not* why I employ you, is it? I employ you for *you* to take the risk, not me ... okay?...if you've got a runner, fine, just make sure he uses *his* car...okay. You know the rules...stick to them."

I wait for another explanation, which I still don't receive. "If it happens again, then the next time you get brought out here, it'll be a different scenario ... okay?" I say sarcastically.

Geezer indicates that he knows I'm serious. And just to put an edge on the moment, so to speak, I pull out the knife, holding it up to his face and letting him look at it for a couple of seconds. His eyes widen, and a concerned expression spreads quickly in his eyes. Holding the cold steel of the six-inch blade to his mouth, I tell him to open it. He doesn't.

"Open your fucking mouth," I demand. "Or I'll cut the fucking thing open."

Slowly with quivering lips and the thoughts of how his smile will be soon be spreading up to his ear, he opens it a little wider, forcing his eyes shut. I carefully put the blade in sideways. "Close your mouth." He slowly closes his mouth, gripping the blade between his trembling lips.

I take his phone out of his pocket.

"Now, make your own way home and I'll speak with you tomorrow, you doss prick!" I say, almost laughing. I know that it'll be no easy feat for him to cut himself out of that lot and then walk the eight miles home.

His body shows signs of relief as he slumps against the tape and breathes out heavily, dribbling snotty bogeys that string down the front of his overfed gut. Prick!

Strolling back to the waiting car where my friend and his friends are, not a word is spoken as I get into the warmth, to the calm sound of the running motor. I close the door and look at my friend.

"All done?" he says with a slight tilt of his head, his eyebrows raised. He doesn't ask for the details.

"Yep, all done" I reply, and he drives me home, dropping me off at my drive. Leaning into the car, I look at them all in turn. "Thanks for your help, gents," I say to them in a genuine tone.

They reply without emotion or expression, in their Polish accents. "No problem, only glad to help"

I look at my friend and offer my hand, which he shakes as I say thanks again.

"Any time," he replies.

The last thing to do is close the door, which I do – firmly, but not to slam. He pulls away with an effortless thrust as the second automatic gear changes up halfway down the road. Making my way to my front door, I watch the foreign plates disappear into the night, knowing the receivers of their next call won't be so lucky.

***

He didn't come to see me after that...he bottled it. So that was the end of that prick. I briefly saw him wandering around town out of his head a few months after that, he looked a right state. Anyway...back to Mack.

Chapter 8

Exploring

The sound of the air con becomes apparent, with Mack's senses coming round as the cool air blows on his legs, waking him. The cotton sheet only just covers his arm, making his body form the foetal position; pulling the sheet fully over him blocks the cold.

Becoming aware of the fact that he's awake, disorientated, and with no idea where he is, his pupils dilate to the brightness of a blurry BBC-news 24 channel, consequently moving shadows loom around the room. The sheets are wet, cold and soggy. Mack's had one of his cold sweats. He only gets them when his subconscious tries to make sense of the death, pain, blood and guts he witnessed while serving with the specials. Where was he for this one? He can't remember; he was asleep.

Sitting on the side of the bed, palms pushing down on the edge of the mattress, he levers himself up and heads towards the shower. A grey, cold ceramic-tiled floor greets his already cold body as he leans into the large silver control-knob located on the wall. Turning it with a now sober hand, warm therapeutic needles of water massage his shoulders and back as he rests his bottom cheeks against the cold tilled wall. Slowly turning the heat adjuster to the correct temperature needed to sooth the now awake mind, life's terms slowly come to the forefront of his thoughts as Mack's now sober, and life's all too real.

A soft towel around his shoulders gives comfort like a baby shrouded by its security blanket, softly sheltering. *Man, I need a drink, a map, and something to eat,* he thinks while picking his shorts off the floor and finding his T-shirt. Still jaded and groggy from the booze and downers he consumed all those hours ago on the flight, he's angry with life. He's angry in having to do the only thing he knows; he wishes he'd taken up another form of accumulating money. The work ahead now takes preference over the easy good-time feelings he had before he lay down. Mack knows it's now time to get organised, and to get a hold on where he is, what things to do next, and in what order.

Being ten fifteen at night, it's time for Mack to check out what Bangkok has to offer, and get his bearings. As he well knows, this is sin city, and by all accounts, as much as he tires of it, this is when Mack comes alive.

As he exits the hotel main doors, for the first time he feels the night time heat. The raw smell of sewage wafts up from the gutters, contorting his face, demanding the release of de-oxygenated breath with a disgusted blow. The heat resembles a Swedish sauna, but without the steam.

"Jeeezaaaz. Doesn't it ever cool down round here? And this place stinks of shit," he says aloud.

Mack knows better; he's been in worse – jungles and all sorts of crap, and he's having a moan about a little night-time heat and the smell of Bangkok. "Pussy," he says to himself.

A voice coming from behind him breaks his thoughts

"Hello!" Mack turns, not expecting to hear a "Hello" in English just outside his hotel. *"What!? It's only the cabby. Has he slept outside the hotel waiting for something or me?*

The cabby waves his wrist at Mack, gesturing him to join him as he pulls over a Thai girl on an old decrepit overstocked push-bike. Buying a clear bag of something, he starts towards Mac with a smile like they're now old friends. As he holds out the bag, he says,

"You li'?"

Mack looks inside and can see the bag contains chopped melon. The cabby proceeds to empty the contents of another bag over the melon: sugar.

Nooooooo, as if melon ain't sweet enough without putting sugar on for Christ sake! he thinks while grimacing.

"No thanks," he says, trying not to offend, but at the same time *not* wanting to try it either.

The cabby looks a little surprised, even a little hurt, so Mack accepts the offer. Skewering a piece with a cocktail stick, he quickly pops it in his mouth and eats it, chomping the sickly substance into a paste before quickly swallowing so the sweetness doesn't have time to make him grimace out loud.

"Mmmmmm," he says to the cabby, nodding his head approvingly, humouring him.

The cabby looks very happy with himself, like he's just opened some brand new experience to Mack. Mack needs to get on. Saying thanks with a smile he starts his walkabout down the street towards what looks like the main road, thinking his glands are going to explode at any second with a sugar overdose.

"I wait," cabby shouts almost excitedly.

Do what you want, Mack thinks, hoping he'll have finished the bag by the time he gets back.

A wave of hustle and bustle greets him as he swans round the corner onto the main drag. He's dodging people just to make headway. It's dark now and busy – very busy. The atmosphere's changed from daytime business to night-time sordidness with testosterone levels at a high. Again, right up Mack's street; however, a map's a priority, so he scans the street for as far as he can see. A shop with a bright red neon sign resembles a convenience store. It's almost amazing that on the other side of the world, he can find a 7-11. It's easily visible among the hundreds of other different coloured signs that beg for trade.

If they haven't a map there, they'll probably know where he could find one. Making his way towards the store, he hears "Hello!" in English. Turning, he sees a well-dressed Thai in an expensive suit calling him over, trying to get him into a suit shop. "No thanks," Mack replies with a smile, thinking he must stand out like a sore thumb.

"Hello, Come, come, come," the Thai persistently demands.

"No thanks," he replies again. "I go there," he says while pointing at the convenience store, and with long strides he walks farther along with his hands in his pockets, dodging people, trying to lose sight of the persistent shop owner.

The convenience store's interior is laced with most things westernised and recognisable, and with prices he understands. A folded up OS map is on prominent display in a rack with loads of others in the corner next to the cold drinks fridge, which sells beers and soft drinks. In addition, on the front of one of the maps, he reads "Bangkok". *Perfect.*

Walking back to the hotel, the suit tries to catch him again.

"No thanks," Mack says again, raising his hand to his ear as if to say "get lost."

Almost back to the hotel, Mack knows that the cabby will be able to give him the reference he needs. When the cabby sees him walking towards the hotel, his eyes light up.

"Okay?" he asks hopefully, looking for some way of selling Mack something else.

"Yeah, where are we?" Mack asks, holding out the map.

"Ah!" says the cabby. He unfolds the map and points at a road on it, which says Sukhumvit, then to a side street where the hotel is.

"Okay," says Mack, now happy he can get his bearings and get on with the organisation of things.

The Thai gestures a hand towards a small restaurant next to the hotel. "Okay," replies Mack again, again being nice. Mack realises that this cabby's only hanging around for him, or so it seems, just to sell him anything he can.

Inside the small restaurant, again he's the only customer; however, again it is a nice place. This time he orders boiled rice with sliced chicken. As before, the cabby sits the other side of the table with nothing to eat, just watching over Mack.

Opening up the map while waiting for the food, he gets accustomed to Bangkok. Tomorrow he has to meet a chap called Ton at the Lumphini stadium. This is where he'll be making the rucksack switch, and get instructions to start what he came out here to do.

Looking up from his thoughts and the map, Mack comes to the conclusion that the cabby's getting tips from wherever he's taken him, which is fair enough as everyone has a family to feed.

Using the paper napkin to clean the tasty food from around his mouth, Mack's now ready to acquaint himself properly with the delights of night-time Bangkok. Offloading the map at the hotel room, and having a quick squirt of antiperspirant, he heads off into the heavy heartbeat and night time sound of a waiting Bangkok.

The aroma of outdoor street stall cooking fills the air as the sky-train rumbles above his head, bringing the presence of him being there into total insignificance within the life of the city. Making a mental note of his surroundings, and making sure he has the hotel's card with him, he heads of for whatever the city of Bangkok is about to bring. The busy road shows makeshift shops, front bars are in abundance. They're everywhere, totally lining both sides of the streets, most with no one sat at them. Walking between street stalls and the shops is the name of the game. Hundreds, thousands of goods are on sale. T-shirts hang in doorways alongside stalls with wooden elephants, wooden ornaments, in fact, wooden everything. There are Rolex watches for a fiver, Ray Ban sunglasses, everything and anything to fill a Sunday trader's pitch, mingled in with music from moody music shops soaking the air with the ambiance of a free-for-all. The carnival atmosphere makes for good sales. The shops and stall keepers try to get Mack to buy something, anything. Mack meanders through, finding his Bangkok legs with a face like a stern donkey, not looking at the goods, because as soon as he does, they will have him.

An open bar further up with dim lights, not looking expensive, beckons him to sit for a drink. A Thai girl sitting behind the wooden bar watches Mack as he saunters up, trying not to look too thirsty. The bar has no frills; it has three fans, one at either end and one behind the bar. There's no back bar or soft drink mixer taps. Just a stand-up bar and chest fridge, which hold the cold liquid to refresh one's thirst. A place to briefly relax, nothing more. *Yep this'll do just fine.*

As he rests himself on a chrome bar stool the Thai girl sees him, opens the chest fridge-freezer from the end of the bar and takes out a folded up white flannel and hands it to him with the usual bowing welcome. Mack knows just what to do with this. Opening it up, he leans his head back and lays the damp cold flannel over his face. *AHHHHHHHHHHHH, sweet relief.* He then moves it to his neck, leaving it there as his body absorbs the cool flush that's flowing through it like a rush. His head drops in relief.

"Sawadeeka," she says, gaining Mack attention.

Looking up at her with a relieved smile of thanks, he says hello.

"You wan' beer?" she asks cheekily, almost provocatively showing off her figure as she turns sideways while keeping her head still and watching Mack's reaction. They all had contacts to a good broad. She checks his eyes to see if that's what he craves; if he does, one will turn up at the bar soon enough to see if she can entertain...at a price.

"Singha, please," replies Mack. He always remembers his manners, and please always seems to do the trick.

A small brown stubby 220ml bottle of Singha is placed on the bar in front of him. She aims the mobile fan at his face. *Nice,* he thinks as he wraps his hand round the cold glass bottle. He lifts his elbow, pouring half the liquid contained in the bottle down his throat without a gulp.

The Thai lady looks at Mack with a pleased expression. "Good?" she asks.

"Lovely," he replies, his eyes watering with relief. She looks confused. "Yeah ... good" he says reassuringly, while holding back a burp.

"Okay," she says as she makes her way slowly over to her friend who's staring at Mack with the baht sign flashing in her eyes. Finishing the bottle he raises it head high to be seen. Another bottle replaces the first and she walks back to talk to chat and laugh with her mate, who's now looking at Mack with a "you're a Farang" look on her round tanned big-lipped Thai face.

Mack's enjoying the buzz around him, watching how the Thais conduct themselves and how the party works. A rather large chap walks up and sits down further along the bar. He's sweating badly while only wearing a cream flannel short-sleeved shirt, cut-off jeans, and black flip-flops. The lady gives him the same treatment, cold flannel, bottle, then a fan pointed at him. Now there's only one fan left; however, there's only one stool left as well.

Mack notices that even though he's speaking Thai, he's definitely English. He sits at the bar with a cigarette sticking out from the corner of his mouth, staring at the lady. Noticing the cigarette coming from his mouth she pulls a Zippo lighter from her jeans pocket, then offers it up once she's sparked it. With that, he grabs the Zippo from her hand and starts to play with it. *Hello?* thinks Mack while watching closely, getting comfortable. The Thai lady walks round the bar and a play fight to get the lighter ensues, Mack watches.

She gets the lighter back after a few squeals of laughter and some body contact, with the chap laughing dirtily.

"They're quite friendly around here then?" Mack says to the chap.

"Yeah, they're okay," he replies, not looking at Mack, and taking a large swig of his booze.

Mack was right; he is English – a northerner by the sound of his accent.

The chap looks over. "Where are you from?" he asks.

"Essex," says Mack. "And you?"

"Manchester."

"Oh right, are you over for a holiday?"

"Well, yeah, sort of. I work on the rigs, so I do three months on, and two months off. Most of my time off I come here" he says, with a 'I've got a great life' attitude.

"I'm only here for a couple of days and then off to Hang Dong," replies Mack. He isn't, he's off to Ko Pang Yang, but the chap doesn't need to know the details.

"Oh, Okay, first time in Bangkok?" he says, looking at the back bar and seemingly bored with the conversation already.

"Yep," says Mack in between drinking his beer.

"Have you tried the Go-Go bars yet?"

"Not yet," he replies with anticipation, waiting for the offer.

"Give us twenty minutes and I'll take you there if you want."

"Yeah, okay," Mack replies, nodding his head, going with the flow.

The big chap takes them to an area just up the road and to the right, then left, straight into a side street that resembles Soho. All the bright colours of Neon lights flash and display silhouettes of provocative poses of females over each entrance. Mack's quite taken aback; he thought that the few dodgy looking places up at Sukhumvit were pretty good, but in this street he wonders if he's going to make it back out alive. The chap directs them to an entrance under a red neon dancing lady. Walking in the dimly lit bar, the atmosphere's heavy with the anticipation of sex. There's suited Chinese men in their dozens, sat down at tables with their eyes glued to an eye-level, T-shaped catwalk. Most are smoking, blowing out plumes that cloud the red and blue lights. The catwalk sports seven Thai ladies parading themselves up and down to the sound of a heavy thumping bass line, wearing just black skimpy G-strings. Clasped between their hands are lit candles, and as if this isn't sexy enough, they're dripping the hot wax over their oiled up, smooth bodies.

"Wow!" Mack says, looking at the chap.

"Yep, this is the place to be," replies his new friend with a wide grin and a wink.

Mack stands there, eyeing the place up. Cigarette smoke rises from every table as the clientele eye up the ladies. They excitedly shout loudly at each other over the sex-charged music.

Two half-dressed ladies approach Mack and his new acquaintance, a twinkle in their eyes make Mack think that the next few minutes could be expensive. They sport fantastic figures with the latest pussy hugging shorts wear; Mack's beginning to feel right at home. They ask what Mack and his new friend want to drink, as the sultry, suggestive universal body language ensues. The chap orders two Singha`s. Two other Thai ladies spot the chap and provocatively make their way over, saying hello, kissing him, rubbing his fat stomach while rubbing their shapely legs on his sweaty freckled white hairy shins. *It's almost like watching something out of a film.*

Again, Mack can see he's in good hands. After a couple of beers, during which his new buddy is constantly approached by the bar girls, Mack asks,

"So how do you get these girls back to the hotel?"

"Just ask them if they want a drink. If they accept, then they like you. After you've chatted 'em up for a while and spent a little money on 'em, ask 'em if they want to go back with you. If they do, they'll ask the top brass. If they come back fully clothed, you've scored and you can take them back."

Easy as that? Mack thinks. *Let's get pissed and enjoy the ambience then.* Mack chooses a lady after a few more beers and plenty of giggling coming from the girls. He does what his new friend advised and she comes back fully clothed. Mack smiles and with a nod and a wink at each other, Mack makes for the exit, with his new mate in tow.

Chapter 9

The Lumphini stadium

Day 2

Again the blowing of the air con wakes him. Feeling the dry soft cotton of the sheets over and below him he realises he's not wet, he didn't have the cold sweats like the day before, but he does feel something new to wake up to, the warmth of a body on his left arm. *Oh yeah*, he thinks, *she stays until 9:00 a.m. and it's only 8.45. Great ... a quickie before she leaves.*

Leaning over, he lovingly removes some hair from the side of her sleeping face. "Morning," he says, watching her wake up and get her bearings.

He shuffles himself off the bed while eyeing up his jeans and money belt; he needs to check, just to make sure all's well. Sleeping with one eye and ear open is something he always does, something he's got used to; you never know ... these girls are good.

The broad wakes up looking tired, Mack looks at her, realising he can't be bothered to make her work for the last of the eight hours he takes fifteen hundred baht out from his money belt, and while handing it to her he tells her to get dressed and go home. She looks at him seemingly concerned, "You no happy?" she asks sheepishly.

"Yeah, I'm happy, I've just got a lot to do today" he replies, like she's now in the way.

She gets the message, quickly getting dressed; again, he receives a personal calling card, looking for that extra feather in her cap. She leaves with a bow and a smile.

Mack checks the Nokia. A message has come through.

:8.30 pm Lumphini stadium, front row, man wearing a white land of soul T-shirt:

Good, he thinks, *we're still in business.*

Beep-beep. Another message comes through. :Taxi man has an empty rucksack. Take to Lumphini for exchange:

Locking the hotel door he makes his way towards the front of the hotel. The cabby from yesterday waits just outside, through the glass doors. Standing outside, the cabby turns around.

"Hello, this fo' you" he says holding out a similar rucksack to the one Mack's already carrying.

Mack returns to his hotel room with the rucksack's strap slung over his left shoulder. Sliding it off once in the room, it bounces onto the bed with the flap facing up. Mack undoes the clasps. In it, there's some tightly rolled fabric weighing about five to seven kilos. *Okay, I know where I'm going, at what time, who to meet, and I've got what I need to take with me. Now we'll see how they operate.*

CNN informs Mack of the time. Checking the Safesnug money belt to make sure he has enough money for the evening, he exits the hotel into the stinking early evening street. Of course, the cabby is waiting for him.

"Where you go?" the cabby asks.

"Lumphini Stadium, please mate." As if the cabby didn't know where he was going.

Twenty minutes later the stadium comes into view. Mack gives the cabby one hundred baht and gets out into the stadium's exterior hustle and bustle. The touts are shouting their ticket advertisings, punters laugh and joke with each other as the buzz engulfs them and their happy groups. An overall sense of excitement fills the air. Mack needs a ticket. Approaching an honest and busy looking tout, he pays fifteen hundred baht for a ringside ticket. The ticket comes with a personal escort who shows him through the main doors into the arena and down to the front, and to his seat.

It's hot, intimidatingly noisy with smoke filling the arena, the atmosphere grows by the minute. The wind and percussion instruments play loudly over the other side of the ring, mingling in well with noisy punters. Snack and drink sellers walk around holding their trays out in front, offering the tasty bagged up, and open products.

The ring's similar to a boxing ring back home, four ropes, a square canvas , a wooden stool in opposite corners of the hard canvas. In fact, except for the chicken wire and weird music, it could be a boxing ring back home; except this isn't boxing ... this is Maui Thai, one of, if not, the hardest fighting sports in the world – a mixture of boxing and other martial arts mixed with years of stamina building and excruciatingly painful exercises.

Mack composes himself as he nestles the rucksack firmly between his feet. A warrior makes his way down the walkway between the excited and respectful crowd, they get to their feet, clapping. The warrior stands on the elevated rim of the ring, holding the ropes. His manager or trainer holds the ropes open for the warrior to enter the battleground. Standing for a couple of seconds to soak up the crowd's appreciation, he confidently climbs through the ropes and onto the canvas, the atmosphere goes crazy filling the stadium with shouts and applauds of respect.

The second warrior makes his way down the walkway and climbs in receiving the same welcome. They wear woven rope headpieces with tail-like tassels. They walk round the ring with gloves in the air, slowly milking the crowd. Once the crowd reach fever pitch the warriors start their ritual dance, bowing and rolling the gloves repeatedly, going down on one knee, rocking back and forth, as they kiss the canvas in each direction. The band gets louder as the ritual progresses and the crowd get rowdier, rising the atmosphere to a now aggressive state. Now we all want the fight to kick off ... and all are gagging for a scrap.

Looking around to see where the heaviest of the atmosphere comes from, it comes from way back behind the chicken wire. The red seats where Mack sits only go eight deep, in two rows of four. Behind these, it elevates by way of concrete steps to rusty old tubular railings. Behind them are long wooden benches. The further back the crowd goes, the rowdier it gets.

The crowd sitting on the front benches are well dressed couples who grow in excitement as the tension builds. However, behind them is what looks like floor to ceiling chicken wire, engulfing the whole circumference of the stadium. Behind the chicken wire is the crowd who make the atmosphere thick with testosterone. They're going bananas, shouting, laughing, milling amongst each other as they're pushed and shoved against the wire. They excitedly wave money around in each other's faces, changing it through clasped hands. Cigarettes dangle from shouting lips; the feeling becomes barbaric.

The fight kicks off. They're a little slow at first, checking each other out through body language and eyeballing, finding the ring space and getting the feel for the canvas. Shouting coming from each of their corners soon forces them to engage each other. The power and stamina of the fighters is incredible. Mack can almost feel the power of the kicks being landed and blocked. The shins, forearms, knees and gloves seem to dish out most of the punishment, while the well-toned bodies absorb it effortlessly. The tempo of the band's volume rises with every knee to the chest and punch to the face, every connection of a spinning back-kick adds fuel to the instruments.

Together with the crowd's chants and shouts, the fight moves up a gear. Mack almost feels like jumping in the ring and having a go. He almost doesn't notice the man wearing a Land of Soul T-shirt who, without looking at him, sits down on the seat to his left. Mack watches the fight until a back-spinning thump lands on the jaw of one of the warriors, sending him to the floor, knocked clean out, as the stadium erupts into a frenzy. Mack claps hard, standing in admiration at such a clean knockout, playing his part in the atmosphere.

The winning warrior gets handed a wad of cash and proceeds to excitedly jump around like a child with a gift he has wanted and received for Christmas. He holds the wad out to the crowd as he jumps almost hysterically on the ropes while shouting something to the crowd. The percussion and wind instrument band dictates the atmosphere; they drop to an ongoing din once the fighter has left the stage and the other comes to his senses, which gives the Thai man a chance to talk.

"You stay just off Sukhumvit in hotel?" he asks.

"Yeah, that's right," Mack replies, knowing this is the contact.

"Taxi-man from hotel brings you here?"

" Yeah, that's right," Mack replies again, not expecting too much conversation.

The Thai gets up and walks off without saying a 'goodbye'. Mack watches him leave with what looks like the rucksack he brought with him. Looking down at an identical one sitting there, he felt the switch, but has to admit, it was pretty good.

It's now time for Mack to leave too as the reasonably smooth and impressive transaction is now complete. Mack now knows he's a target, but for who? He only knows of one; however, there may be others and now he wants to get away. Knowing things of great value are with him of course breeds a lot more self-awareness and paranoia.

Outside, as usual, the cabby waits among the fast-paced street and city sounds.

"Okay?" the cabby asks with a smile, eyebrows raised.

"Yeah, great!" Mack replies remembering the fight he's just watched with great respect.

The cabby drives him back to the hotel and with a typical Thai bow says goodnight. In the relative safety of the hotel room his next move is to make a phone call. Using the Nokia is a little dodgy because it may be traced. Leaving the hotel in search of a pay phone, Mack's glad the cabby knocked off early. Walking down the main drag, he finds the convenience store he'd previously bought the map from and buys a phone card. Finding a payphone, he dials the number he memorised.

"Hello," says the voice on the other end.

"Glue," Mack replies.

"All okay?" replies the voice.

"Good as gold, the switch has been made. I'll contact you when I have new instructions," says Mack and puts the phone down.

Mack, being part of a three-team operation has to call in when need be to inform his team of progress. There's the head, who deals with the intelligence; the fixer, who takes care of the surrounding obstacles (who Mack just spoke to) and then there's Mack, the field operative who does all the dirty work.

If they can find the underlying cause of this ring and draw out the hit man named Christophe, who by the way carries a healthy £1.000,000 price on his head – dead or alive – then they all stand to get £33,330 each, 10% of the bail money. Not bad for a couple of week's work ... not bad at all.

You see, Mack and his team are no messing, do what others won't do, go where others won't go freelancers ... bounty hunters.

Chapter 10

The Danube Basin

Day 3

The sea vixens roar from over a mile away as they fade off into the distance, returning to the Ark Royal.

Going over the ridge of the basin, looking into the bowl, the glow of stubble, what's left of the crop, brightens up as the wind blows brashly over – nature not giving a second thought.

Not a sound from feet, breath, hardware, nothing. Just the stench of Napalm. The stench of gel mixed with the fuel and JP-5...bad fucking news.

A smouldering mess of unrecognisable pieces. Annihilation. The smell's unbearable. The Radfan rebels have gone. White compounded mud bricks, other shit which made up the village and the community – black, dormant, burnt, scattered, truly fucking done. The still coma of death surrounds every sense, getting into every pore.

No bodies. The Radfan rebels knew we were coming, looks like they've been gone for a long time. Absolute anni-fuckin-hilation. The Yemen border; they've gone there.

Something's not right here. Something ... is so not fucking right here.

A smell, not Napalm. What the fuck is it? Where the fuck's that smell coming from?

All clear, I know it's all fucking clear, you cunt. I just fucking told you that. Fucking hand signals, not fucking smoke arm signals, o-fucking-kay!

A ghost walking up to the top of a brick well. The smell's getting stronger, something ain't fuuuuckiiiiing riiiiiiight ...

A draw of breath like he's just surfaced from deep water, pours into Mack's mouth. The sheets are soaked. He's drenched. The electric fuzz ... the echo of his brain coming to its senses is all too much.

Mack sits on the side of his bed with his head in his hands, crying like a deeply torn soul. The visions of those dead villagers down the well ... children. Mack's angry. Mack is so angry. He still can't comprehend why they did that. They could have polluted the wells some other way. The eyeballs in his sockets thrash from side to side as the fury grows. Mack wants to release his anger.

Starting with that fucking chair against the door. The bed goes upside down. The phone goes through the window. The wardrobe doors are ripped from their hinges, forced into the shower cubicle, smashing the mirror and shower head. A cabinet, thrown against the wall, disintegrating into three chunky pieces...

Visions of terror in the child's eye makes him want to scream through his blood-shot tear-soaked eyes. His rampage won't go outside his mind or body; it's not allowed to. Restraining his inner matter, bringing his actions to a halt, he looks around at the untouched room, knowing that *their* pain is over.

This somehow gives a relief from the anger, as he knows that peace and tranquillity will also be his ... one day.

Mack pulls his shit together and runs a shower. He just hopes no one pisses him off today. *Fuck it!!!*

Chapter 11

Destination Koh Phangan

Mack's washed and dressed, feeling almost normal again as he exits the reception of the hotel. He's going to need another rucksack, a slightly bigger one that'll hold the cargo and his personal belongings. He checks the phone for a message:

"Had Sadet, shark bar @ 1.30pm, Koh Phangan, 2 days."

Okay, he thinks. *First things first: a ticket and a slightly larger rucksack.*

The cabby catches Mack as he leaves the hotel shouting "Hello!" – probably wanting to sell him something or take him somewhere to spend some money.

Mack replies with an "All right, mate," while strolling off towards the main drag to find the travel agent he noticed the day before. It's only two minutes away. The travel agents seem to be very well organised with all the necessary hardware, such as fax machines and computers, etc. Even the chairs are comfy-looking with their thick black-plastic frames and red spongy seats.

"Sawadeeka." A lady in a full green uniform looking like an air hostess greets him, bowing. She gestures to a chair for him to sit.

"Hello," he replies.

"Hello. What can we do for you?" she asks.

"A ticket to Koh Phangan."

"Okay. How you go?" she asks pointing to pictures of a plane, train and coach.

"Coach," he says pointing to the picture.

"Okay, when?"

"Today."

"Okay," she says and starts plugging away on the desktop computer. "Today at nineteen thirty hours?" she says, turning the screen in Mack's direction.

"Yeah, okay. That'll be fine,"

She babbles on about how he changes at Surat Thani and then gets the boat to Koh Phangan and a cab to where he's now booked in for one night, all included in the price. *Great, no problems,* he thinks. "How much?" he asks.

"920 baht," she says, pointing out the prices.

Leaving the agents and in his Safesnug money belt, he has a ticket for a coach, then a boat and a one-night stay at his final destination, Koh Phangan.

Collecting his personal belongings from his hotel, he checks out. As usual, the cabby's there, trying to get Mack's attention by repeating the word "hello."

"Later," Mack replies, raising a hand without looking at him and wandering off.

He's got eight hours before his coach leaves. *So plenty of time to buy a new rucksack and a drink,* he thinks rubbing his hands together in approval of the relaxation that a few bottles of Singha will bring.

Fifteen beers, four or five open front bars, and some food off the street later, he makes his way back to the hotel front with the new rucksack purchased earlier from the shop on the corner. She showed him a strange ritual of flicking the baht over as many goods she had on display as she could apparently this brings good sales to the day.

A little unsteady on his feet from the afternoon's drinking session, he approaches the cabby who's still outside the hotel and points at the ticket, asking for directions.

"Oh!" the cabby exclaims, putting his hands on his head in horror.

"What?" Mack asks feeling concerned.

The cabby then starts shouting at another cabby who comes over. The cabby shows him the ticket, the other cabby copies what the last cabby did, putting his hands on his head with a look of panic while saying something quickly in Thai. The other Thai fumbles around for his phone flicking it open. This starts to unsettle Mack who by now wants to know what the hell's going on.

On the phone the cabby's talking fast to someone. Bringing the phone away from his ear he says to Mack in a stern voice,

"You wait!"

Mack's cabby tries to explain to him that he doesn't have time to get to the coach meeting point by cab. He only has three-quarters of an hour before the coach's departure and it's rush hour. There's no way he'll make it half way across Bangkok in the rush hour.

Shit! thinks Mack. He's been drinking all afternoon and just took it for granted that the coach meeting point was somewhere local to the estate agents.

A few minutes later, a motor bike roars up the side street, pulling up to the cabby, he and the Thais have a quick shouting conversation with them all seemingly to agree on something. The cabby tells Mack to get on. *Fair enough*, he thinks and gets on the back. The rider puts a helmet on Mack's head, does it up, and re-mounts.

The cabby has a quick chat with the rider, who's already revving the bike to an uncomfortable volume, and says goodbye to Mack, slapping the helmet goodbye. Mack thanks the cabby for everything he's done for him during his short stay and the bike takes off with the front wheel nearly of the ground demanding Mack to grab the back grab-bar with his ankles uncomfortably up almost by his ears.

Luckily for Mack he's ridden pillion before. However, this rider's taking no prisoners as he flies down the five-lane main road five times faster than the seven-or eight-mile-an-hour average speed of the other oncoming traffic in the rush hour. They weave in between cars, taxis, tuk-tuks, other bikes – and all the while it's getting dark.

Lean left, lean left again, then right. He's on a ride that won't stop except by meeting another solid obstacle or reaching their destination. *This is one hairy ride!!* Mack thinks, while breathing in to zoom between oncoming hooting vehicles and the central reservation.

Horns are sounding everywhere as they weave in and out of oncoming and forward moving vehicles. Brake lights are flashing through red lights, green lights, people shouting. *This is one fucking hairy ride!* Mack thinks again. *This man's a bloody expert at riding, and he knows his way around Bangkok too ... Shiiiiit!*

Mack knows this is a race against time to catch his coach. *Jesus Christ! We only just missed that one!* he thinks as the material of his jeans touch a car on the way past. This happens a good few times as Mack tries his damndest to imitate a bean pole before reaching their destination.

As the pandemonium slows, the rider pulls off the main highway and down a side street leading to the coach stop. The bike slows to a standstill outside a busy terminal. People stand with their luggage piled up beside the road, waiting. The rider plants his feet either side of the bike for Mack to get off. In the transit Mack's legs have turned to jelly, which is quite noticeable to anyone watching as he dismounts the idle sounding motor bike, a little wobbly. *Pussy!* he thinks to himself.

The rider seems very pleased with himself as Mack unfastens the strap on the helmet and slides it off. The rider indicates that this is the place he needs. Mack's pretty impressed too giving the rider two hundred baht for his efforts. The rider's over the moon with his payment and with a helmet muffling yahoo, he revs off up the road ... this time actually doing a wheelie, leaving Mack with his rucksack laughing out loud, agreeing with the rider's enthusiasm.

Checking his watch to see if there's any time for a beer, a welcome long hand on the watch gives the thirst-quenching answer needed. *Ten minutes left yet.* He spots an empty stool at the open-front bar only ten feet away... *That will do just fine.*

The cold flannel sits around his neck with the rucksack snugly around his foot. The Singha's cold and this bar plays music. 'Yeke Yeke' by Mory Kante booms out to a now relaxed persona.

Ordering a couple of bottles for the journey, a Turkish chap also orders a couple. *Now then, Turks in Thailand are very rare. An amazing coincidence considering the contact is a Turk,* he thinks as his mind starts to race. *Is this Turk a plant to keep an eye on me? Or something else? If he is... then how did he follow me here so quickly?*

Mack knows his journey here didn't waste a second. So how could someone follow him here, unless he knew what bus he was catching from the tourist booth?

Okay. This is fine. I've stuck to what I'm supposed to do, so I shouldn't be looking dodgy. Then he remembers the phone call he made to his team yesterday. *Shit, don't tell me they bugged the phone? No, don't get paranoid. They wouldn't know which phone I was going to use, even if I was to make a phone call. Anyway, there's nothing I can do now except keep going through the motions of not knowing what the hell I'm doing and act as if I'm just out to earn a few bob. I don't know what the cargo is, do I? ... The trouble is, I do know what I'm carrying, and I know what it's worth.*

Mack has to be cool. If he makes a wrong move, gives the game away, then making the correct contacts and winding his way into the 'circle', drawing out the hit-man, will be out of the window. Not only that, Mack will be dead.

Mack keeps his eye on the Turk as they all board the bus, watching closely to see where he sits. The Turk sits downstairs, where the round table and comfy circular bench seats are. Mack goes upstairs near the back. Now he's on his guard, he wants to keep an eye on the comings and goings of the stairwell. Not only that, being near the emergency exit gives for an ... emergency exit. The seats are reasonably comfortable, with arm rests and a foot rest, and not only that, he has a seat by the window.

Day 4

After what seems like a lot longer than fourteen hours later, with only two stops to break the monotony of a droning engine which is right below him, they arrive at Surat Thani, just as light starts to break. The atmosphere is idyllic, with the sky a deep orangey red. The brightest star or two can still be seen, and a few stray clouds can just be made out by their dark silhouettes; they'll burn off as soon as the sun hits them. It's a perfect part of the world, with the temperature at a cosy warmth.

Waiting for the boat in a very large-purpose wooded area just off from the water's edge, people gather in twos and threes. Single people wander around stretching their legs. The waiting area resembles a large open-plan restaurant, except it shows the characteristics of a McDonald's. This is a large shelter with toilets, all made from rough wood. The food servery has shutters, which are closed; however, there are large lit-up vending machines that can only just be seen behind the queue as the thud of purchased items land in the tray.

The plastic seats and tables are fixed to the ground, and are all taken up. This place could hold a few hundred people or so. Not a long wait, because the boats sail at approximately 8:30. The Turk seems to have disappeared, taking the edge off things for the moment. Mack sits patiently with the cargo. People talk to each other and laugh. Some have their Thai phrase books out, testing each other, while others are drinking cans of Thai lager while milling around looking at their flip-flops – all in all, a happy holiday atmosphere.

Mack has the opportunity to change into the flip-flops and shorts he bought earlier while shopping for a larger rucksack. The atmosphere goes from a low din to a little busier. People start to gather their things and head towards the wooden jetty. Mack looks around. *Yep, time to go.*

Following the crowd to where they board, the Turk comes into view just as Mack's negotiating the narrow gangplank. He watches the Turk closely to see where he goes. He goes to the air-con area in the centre of the boat, which has seats and a TV. Mack goes to the back of the boat; again, he has a good view of what's occurring in front and around him.

The boat sets sail. Its mainly manned with English, Americans and Germans, judging by what languages Mack can overhear. Most look like travellers, what with their braided or plaited hair and colourful clothing. There's no room for a dog, almost overcrowded, the only part of the boat that can be seen is the top being the captain's cabin, one level up. The bodies of people trying to get comfortable, lying down, dangling their legs over the side or sitting cross-legged, completely cover the surface of the boat.

The repetitious chugging sound slowly becomes unheard as it blends into the new day. Fish dart from the clear and perfectly blue water, skipping over the water's surface alongside, and in front of the vessel as if to accompany them, or even race them. The skipping fish let the boat know who's boss of the ocean, then when they've made their point, they disappear into the smooth blue water.

The sun, now high burns hot on white flesh while the breeze slightly cools. People rummage around in bags and pockets to find suntan lotion; no one wants to be burnt before arriving on some of the most beautiful islands on the planet – they can do that once they get there.

Three hours or so later the port of Koh Samui welcomes the holidaymakers; it's another small island that looks like something out of a magazine: perfect, fine sandy beaches with palm trees and no high buildings. Mack wants to get off here, but he can't; business is business.

Mack looks closely at the gangplank, watching to see if the Turk gets off. He does, giving slight relief to a slowly building tension. The boat sets sail again, leaving the Turk and Mack's edginess behind. An hour later, they dock at Thong Sala, Koh Phangan.

Finding his feet on solid ground, Mack needs a cab to take him to the place he'll be staying at; Mae Haad.

A 4x4 silver flat bed with bench seats in the back advertising Mae Haad and a couple of other destinations on the island gives Mack a clue that it might be the cab he needs. He shows his ticket to the driver, who waves his hand for Mack to get on the back. Once the bench seats are full and people are hanging off the metal frame that loops the back of the truck, they set off. It's a bumpy ride that lasts for forty-five minutes and has three stops. Mack's seen some beautiful locations in his time, but at each stop they seem to get better. Mack's is the last stop.

A fantastic bay greets him. As the sound of the 4x4 fades, tranquillity overpowers all his senses as he stands and stares at the view, taking in the beauty of this small out of the way non-English picture-postcard resort.

Palm trees stretch up high, leaning towards the ocean, as a slight warm breeze gently blows through their giant leaves. White powdery sand covers everything around him, stretching its warm soft arms towards the shallow light-blue water. No sun loungers, frisbee, cricket, football, or topless ladies frequent this beach, which is deserted and unspoilt, topping all beauty. Mack's going to like it here.

A clatter of cutlery diverts his attention further up and to his right; the wooded building boasts a large wooden sign with the same name that's on his travel documents, and under it the word, in English, "Reception" A restaurant sprawls to a large reception desk. To the left of this, back near the glistening sea's edge along the bank, small huts on stilts sit looking at the water. Small two-man fishing boats float near the water's edge, moored near some brown rocks. Mack breathes a heavy sigh of wonder and peace at this almost magical destination.

Six red 125cc scooters stand up in a line, with the front wheels all turned to the left. A "Rent" sign hangs above them.

The light sand flicks up the back of his legs as he makes his way to the slightly cooler reception area. Large ceiling fans slowly turn as the four-foot-high counter with leaflets, menus and maps greets him.

"Sawadeeka," says a short dark tanned Thai lady, who stands behind the counter. She bows and smiles.

Mack says, "Hi," as he digs around in the Safesnug for the required paperwork and passport for his stay. He's only booked for one night so he asks, "How much for three nights?"

She explains that all the huts are the same price. Mack pays for three nights stay; 360 baht in total. He's shown to his hut by the more than happy middle-aged lady who leaves the key, and of course gives a complementary bow.

The hut stands on its stilts in the corner of the coved beach just up from the rocks. A red hammock swings from the small man made looking veranda's supporting cross beams, looking secure and comfortable. Inside a double bed and a ceiling fan furnish the room. To the left of the bed is the door to the floor-to-ceiling tiled bathroom. No frills, just a toilet, and a shower handle coming out of the wall. Mack's arrived. He now needs a shower, food and – of course – a beer.

***

Shit! I'm really starting to need that piss now!... it's sidetracked my concentration. I'm looking at the counter watching Geezer walk off with a book of first class stamps, which leaves another window empty. I wait for the queue to shorten but it doesn't. In fact, when I glance as far back as I can, the queue stretches round the corner and out of sight, at least another ten people have joined, giving to an inpatient atmosphere.

Now then... I see a woman asking for an application form for a passport, as far as I can remember she made a bit of a name for herself in the local boozer a while ago. (She's a little twisted)

She's not aware of what people think of her, but if she did know, it would probably start so much trouble, that they'd do better by keeping their thoughts to themselves. By all accounts she did a bit of a dirty on one of her so called friends, it was quite a while ago now, however, she did it, and as far as I'm concerned she can't be trusted.

Her name is Trudy.. and the friend she did the dirty on was a long time friend of hers by the name of Ted. The thing is Ted and Trudy had almost grown up together, their boyfriends and girlfriends were good friends too, so they spent quite a bit of time in the same circle.

As the years had gone by a deeper bond of friendship had forged between them, but Ted had found himself in a serious relationship with another girl, and Trudy was no longer involved in his life...so as to speak, Trudy didn't like this...so set about earning herself a reputation...and this is how it went.

Chapter 12

Clever girl (Part 1)

Trudy makes a point of bumping into Ted's girlfriend down the town while on a shopping trip, you know...

"Oh, hi Helen!" she shouts while running across the road, almost falling over herself to get to her. While they're having their chat and Trudy's sussing Ted's girlfriend out, she starts boasting about how well she knows Ted, better than anyone else in fact, including Ted's girlfriend Helen. Well, of course Ted's girlfriend Helen knows about his murky past, but he has been going out with her now for nearly a year without any hiccups, so of course she defends him to the end by saying,

"Ted's changed, he doesn't do coke any more, he hardly goes out and splits his time between work and me."

This of course, adds insult to injury and winds Trudy right up.
1. Ted doesn't go round to Trudy's any more,
2. Ted isn't wasting money and time on cocaine any more, which is a problem for Trudy because she can't stop doing the stuff, she's too busy keeping up appearances, doing what everyone else still does and...
3. How dare someone else get to know Ted better than she does, have control over him, considering the amount of time Ted and Trudy have known each other, and what's more by all accounts they seem to be having a happier relationship than the one she has with her boyfriend.

"Fuck, fuck, fuck!" she thinks in her warped mind.
"I know what, I'll fuck them both up, at the same time making it look like I'm doing Helen a favour. Then...I'll look good, Ted will look bad, I'll be back in charge, and all will be back to normal; that should do the trick." So she says to Ted's girlfriend,

"I don't think you know Ted as well as you think you do."

Ted's girlfriend looks confused. "What do you mean?" she asks.

"Well okay, so Ted's off the coke, and he seems happy with your relationship and all that, but I reckon if he was given half the chance he'd shit on you without a second thought."

Ted's girlfriend can`t believe she`s hearing this. "Eh? What do you mean?"

"Well, if I was to invite Ted round to our place one evening, I bet he'd shit on you before the night's out."
Helen is still not believing what she's hearing coming from Trudy's mouth. "No way!" she shouts.
"Okay," says Trudy. "Let me invite him round for a night and we'll see. Don't say anything to him about the fact that you've seen me...and we'll see, okay?"
Helen doesn't like this at all, however the seed's now sown, and she agrees with Trudy that just to prove Trudy wrong about Ted, she'll go along with it.

So Trudy rushes home and persuades her husband to phone Ted, invite him over next Saturday night, they'll tell him that Bindi (who Ted had fancied for years) will be there, and there'll be plenty of coke, you know...a harmless friendly coke night.

So he's on the phone to Ted telling him about the personal invite; they're going to have a small, select party. But Ted doesn't really want to go, he hadn't done any coke for nearly a year now and doesn't really have any interest in a party round there, or an interest in Bindi any more, for that matter. Trudy's husband detects this in the conversation, so quickly changes the reasons for wanting him to come round. Ted still knows people who deal in coke, and claims that he doesn't have any more, so needs Ted to organise things.

"Okay," says Ted, a little reluctantly, "I'll see what I can do."
He agrees to meet them at their place at 8.30 pm on a Saturday night. The phone call ends, and the plan's hatched.

Trudy then phones Ted's girlfriend, proceeding to tell her that he's coming round there next Saturday night and.... will sort out the drugs.

"Ted's supplying them!" Trudy exclaims, pretending she's shocked too. She then carries on winding Helen up by telling her that Bindi's going to be there too, and Ted knows that. Of course Helen's gutted to hear this, but Helen didn't know about Ted having a thing for Bindi in the past, however she does now...and the fire is growing within Helen.

Over the next few days, Helen asks Ted what he's doing next Saturday night. Of course Ted doesn't want his girlfriend to know he's scoring some coke for Trudy, her husband and their buddy Bindi, then going round Tony and Trudy's for the night, does he? Ted would look like the bloke he used to be a couple of years ago, a coke-taking womaniser. Ted doesn't want to ruin his relationship but at the same time doesn't want to let down his old buddies. So he's in a bit of a conundrum. He of course tells her a white lie, saying that he's off out with some old friends for the evening. Ted hasn't lied, he just hasn't told the whole truth. The trouble is that by now he's starting to look like a very bad boy. However, he hasn't done the dirty deed... yet, he could still pull out at any time, but Ted being Ted, he doesn't want to let his friends down, he just thinks it's going to be a pleasant evening in with some `old skool` friends mulling over how things have been over the last year or two, with no repercussions. How wrong could Ted be? How stitched up is he?

Helen phones Trudy when she gets a chance, agreeing that maybe she doesn't know Ted as well as she thought she did, and maybe the future isn't as safe as she thought with Ted, of course Trudy loves this, she's already rocked the boat and Ted hasn't even done anything yet. As usual Ted's getting himself into trouble by doing other people favours. It couldn't be going better for Trudy, she's been waiting for this chance for ages.

So Trudy goes a little deeper, "Tell you what, if things do start to get a little heated on Saturday night, just so you can see that I'm not lying about it, I'll phone you and you can come round, look through the curtains and see for yourself what's going on."

If there's one thing that Trudy's good at, it's how to keep an audience. She's more than capable of keeping it all happening in the living room for as long as she likes, which of course happens to be downstairs at the front of the house, an easy place for Helen to peek through the curtains.

Trudy explains that the curtains will be pulled shut, but not quite together, open just enough for Helen to be able to see through from outside. Oh yes, Trudy is the true game master.

"Okay" Helen says, not very happy, but agreeing to wait for the phone call on Saturday night.

The atmosphere changed between Ted and Helen during that week, and in all honesty, Ted should have picked up on it, however Ted, not wanting to think that he was being paranoid, ignored the alarm bells.

***

Anyway, I'll carry on with this one in a bit, back to Mack and his new island of beauty.

Chapter 13

The Turks

Day 5

Mack wakes, scratching his mosquito bitten legs in the stiflingly hot room. The sweat that oozed from him in his overheated slumber soaks in as its quickly absorbed by the clean cotton sheets. A lazy evening of watching the sun slowly turn a hazy red was enjoyed the night before, as he had lain in his hammock listening to the sounds of the night, recumbent and slowly lubricating his throat with a few bottles of Singhas, straight from the brightly lit fridge.

Today he's going to need his trainers, because today he's going to meet the contact further around the island at Had Sadet. Emerging into the heat and glare of the Mae Haad bay looking for breakfast, he stops on the hut's veranda sitting on his rented hammock, tacking in the morning's surroundings, truly enjoying his stay. The etching sound of a loan cricket in the otherwise soundless air adds to the ambience of the morning's beauty. Mack glances over to the small, idyllic-looking island just off shore. When the tide's low a sand walkway that connects the two can be seen. Mack decides he's going to go snorkelling around it after his meeting – check out the coral, take in the local marine life, relax a little more.

The reception area is a cooler temperature than the outdoors, which is refreshing as he isn't wearing a sun hat yet. Waiting at the wooden bar area, he remembers helping himself to the cold bottles of Singha kept in the tall glass fridge last night. So long as he put the bottle tops in the basket, they'd bill him for them today, which Mack thinks is a good way of doing things.

The Thai lady comes out with a "Sawadeeka" and the same routine: a smile and a bow.

"You pay for beer?" she asks.

"Yeah, and could I rent a bike please?"

"Okay, 300 for beer ... ah, 180 baht for the bike, and we hold your passport," she says.

Mack glances at how many bottle tops there are in the basket and wonders if he had a drink with anyone else last night.

"I'm going to need my passport for later, when I change a traveller's cheque," Mack replies, not wanting to leave his passport with anyone.

She gives him back his passport and lets him know that a deposit will be needed instead of his passport. He gives her a $50 traveller's cheque.

They walk to the bikes and she puts the keys into a side lock on the down bar, clicking the lock she turns the handlebars and presses the orange button on the right next to the twist back accelerator. The bike's electronic ignition kicks in and the bike's running to a well balanced tick over.

"Thank you," Mack says, jumping on with a smile and a wink, fully up for a spin.

He twists the handgrip back lunging the scooter forward. Taking it a little easy at first because of the lightly sand-covered and skiddy surface, and with feet pointing out, he cautiously makes his way to the main road. With the rucksack firmly attached to his back, and in his cut down well-fitting jeans and an open neck short-sleeved shirt, he feels good.

The main drag is nothing more than a wider piece of tarmac, but a lot less sandy, he turns left, and leaning forward opens the throttle to full capacity. The automatic bike picks up quickly for a small engine, reaching sixty miles per hour in no time. The feeling of the controlled speed and sound of wind rushing past his ears is an experience that he'd forgotten about, bringing back memories that make his trip a little more real.

Passing a small sign that says "Ban thong" a little further along, he can see a small coastal village. He reaches it and pulls in. The noise comes to a stop, leaving the whole area remarkably quiet. Leaving the bike on its stand near an open-front refreshment bar that advertises Chang, he makes his way to it. The round metal tables have small round brown glass ashtrays on them, and the place is empty. *Nice... I've got a couple of hours before I meet the contact, so I may as well enjoy the peace and quiet, and get acquainted.* Mack orders the brew.

A cold bottle's put on the bar. No cold flannels or fans at his face here though. Half way through the drink, he watches as a black 4x4 pull up next to his parked bike.

Two Turks get out. Mack can't believe his eyes. One of them's the one on the boat yesterday.

well this could be interesting, he says to himself sarcastically.

They look at him as they walk into the sparse bar area. Going straight to the bar, they immediately start talking quickly and quietly to each other. Mack feels that something's about to kick off... and to be fair, he doesn't want to be sitting down for it. Slowly rising from the stool, he stands at the bar with them to his right, making room between himself and the stool, just in case he needs the room to manoeuvre.

Mack notices that one of the Turks is touching the outside of his front waistband area through his shirt as he orders lemonade. The rucksack has a centre clasp as well as shoulder straps, so he can move freely if need be without losing the sack.

Are the keys in my pocket or in the bike? Shall I just make a move and go? Or wait and see what happens? Mack decides to go, get away from any problems that may arise.

As leisurely as anyone else would, he finishes the drink and makes his way out using his peripheral vision as he leaves. The Turks' conversation stops as the atmosphere tenses. The keys dangle from the down bar of the bike for an easy start-up. Flicking the key to the on position and pushing the starter, it revs into action. Shifting the bike off its stand Mack glances towards the Turks as he turns it round, and revs off back to the main drag. The Turks hadn't moved.

Feeling happy with the fact that he easily got out of a possibly awkward situation, he checks his mirrors; the black 4x4 is approaching fast judging by the sand it's kicking up from behind. His heart starts to race as thoughts pound his senses. For no real reason at all Mack feels like he's being chased. However, panic never did anyone any good, so he carries on rather than pulling over.

The 4x4 in his mirrors gets closer and slows down behind him, as if waiting for another vehicle to pass in the other direction before overtaking; suddenly it pulls round and roars past and into the distance. Mack's heart's now showing signs that his mind started the adrenaline pump and put him into a state of readiness – and ready he is.

Five minutes further on the dusty road, the black 4x4 can be seen pulled over to the side of the road. Mack instinctively has a quick glance around at his surroundings, nothing but trees lining the road with sand and sticks. His concentration shifts back to the pulled-over 4x4, the gut feeling he's having isn't a good one, not liking it at all. It's too late, the bike's front wheel jams into a pothole he hadn't anticipated jerking the handlebars from his grip. The momentous force throws him forward as the bike almost starts its crash manoeuvre, Mack's in mid air. Instinctively like a cat, he manages to manoeuvre himself into a controlled somersault, so as to land on his back – on the rucksack, taking the sting out of the fall, then forward onto the seat of his jeans sliding with legs stretched out and apart for balance. The sound of the metal and plastic of the bike scraping on the tarmac, sliding on its own momentum behind him makes him aware he has a heavy object closing in fast. The object stops, Mack stops, the noise stops. A cloud of sandy dust envelops him, the 4x4 just ahead still sits with its engine idle.

Through the sandy dust one of the Turks urgently makes his way over, Mack clocks the other Turk by a tree. The wind blows the shirt of the Turk up slightly showing a P14 flashing in the sun. Mack knows it's a P14 because he knows its younger brother, a Kimber 1911. He can recognise these babies at a glance.

Quickly turning himself onto all fours as the Turk gets in range Mack launches himself up and, using his upward momentum lifts his right leg, turning his foot inwards so as to expose the heel, he thrusts his bodyweight right with arms counter balancing. His heel swings out catching the Turk square on the jaw. Crack! The Turk goes down with a heavy thump, knocked clean out.

The other Turk's seen what's happened and starts running over with – believe it or not – a Kimber in his hand, pointing it at Mack's gut. Within a small distance he'll be in range too. Mack takes one stride forward landing himself in knife-hand back-stance. In one fluid movement he grabs the gun using a knife-hand palm strike to the inside of the barrel, twisting the gun outwards and away from the firing line, it twists out of the Turk's hand, into Mack's. A knee full force finds its target: the groin. The Turk goes down unarmed, curled up and clutching his groin, pain flashing through his wide open popping out eyes as the mouth opens fully for a sharp intake of air.

Mack wastes no time for a conversation. Tucking the 1911 down the back of his jeans, he grabs the bike which is still on the ground with the back wheel slowly turning, pulling it upright. He jumps on and revs off up the road, leaving the Turks on the ground.

Mack arrives at Had Sadet. The shark bar, which is on the main drag and where he's supposed to be meeting his contacts, its easily found as it has a huge great painting of a great white down the full length of one side. Parking the damaged but still in good nick bike down a side street, he hitches it onto the sand and turns it off. The last five minutes proceedings seems to now take a back seat of surealeality, as the relaxed ambience of the area plays its part. This time the keys stay with Mack. Strolling back round the corner and into the shark bar, he orders a Singha, calms himself, and waits for his contacts.

Chapter 14

Bodyguards

With his eyes fixed firmly on the entrance and his back to the wall, his adrenaline finds a happy medium while the mind re-organises itself, finding that place of pure alertness... just in case of more action.

Ten to fifteen minutes later, the roar of a 4x4 can be heard. Mack hears it pull up outside the bar with a dry-sand skid. He's tucked the bike away down a side street so as not to be seen.

Trust me to go to a bar that they obviously use.

So Mack's back to square one again; the Turks didn't have to look far for him, he's gone straight to their bar...*Prat! Okay, at least they know I'm not to be messed with and the fact that I have one of their guns may slow them down a little, rather than straight into another fight. I have the upper hand because they don't know I'm here, well not until they see me anyway, and it's too late for an exit...so let's see what happens.*

Having checked that the mag holds ammo when got of the bike, he points the gun towards the door from under the table that he's sat at, he's as ready as he'll ever be, so takes a long, slow swig of the booze with his empty hand, keeping a close eye on the door.

The Turks slowly enter the bar, clocking Mack straight away. Mack makes a slight but sudden move to see how the land lies. Both the Turks immediately jump into action, standing bolt upright, shouting with their hands out, legs apart, knees slightly bent. They lean forward with arms out and palms up in the "STOP" sign.

"No, Mr Mack! No, no. We're supposed to be meeting *you* here. It's us, we are your contacts. It's okay!"

Mack doesn't say anything. He's listening, checking their body language, seeing how they *really* are. They're submissive, panicky, concerned.

"Okay, so why were you pulled over ready to jump me back there?" Mack says in a cool tone, eyebrows raised, waiting for an explanation.

"We weren't," one of the Turks quickly blurts out. "My brother needed the toilet, so we stopped for him go. He was taking one up against the tree. You came off your bike, so I came over to help. You then knocked me out, and my brother saw what was happening and came over to help me, and you kneed him in the groin."

"Fuck me... I thought you two were a couple of wide boys trying it on," Mack replies, almost laughing.

"No, no, Mr Mack," they reply, relieved that Mack's listening.

Mack pauses for a second. "You'd better take a seat then," he says, kicking the chairs out from under the table for them to sit on.

The Turks look at each other, relief written all over them. Still a little uncertain, they slowly make their way to the table and carefully sit down without taking their eyes off Mack, angry with the fact that he has just caused considerable pain to them, but at the same time...a little wary.

"Drink?" Mack asks sarcastically, tilting his head slightly to the right.

"Lemonade for both of us please, thanks," the Turk replies appreciatively.

Mack arrogantly shouts over to the Thai bar man for a Singha and two lemonades with ice.

"My name is Ennis, and this is my brother Ali," Ennis says, now trying to be business-like.

Oh great, thinks Mack. *Penis and Ally fucking Ba-Ba,* he chuckles to himself. "Hello, Ennis; Ali," he says with a grin, holding his hand out to be shaken.

They both dubiously shake his hand, looking him straight in the eye. The Thai brings the drinks over. Mack gives him a note and tells him to keep the change.

"Okay, so what happens next?" Mack asks.

"Have you got the plates?"

"In the sack," Mack replies.

"Now we have to go to Haad Rin and deliver it, so you come with us?" Ennis asks quite politely.

"Yeah, no problems, now I know who you are. I've just got to get the keys from the bike," Mack replies.

"Okay thank you, we'll wait here," says Ennis.

Mack retrieves his keys and returns to the bar. They finish their drinks and set off in the 4x4.

Mack's sandwiched between the Turks for the journey. The trek to Haad Rin is a little bumpy to say the least. The single pot-holed road at one stage is at such a steep gradient that Mack thinks there's a possibility of the 4x4 going back on its back wheels and flipping straight over.

Turning off the main drag the 4x4 does what it's supposed to do, dealing with a very pot holed and uneven sandy track, lined with tall palm trees. The trees slowly give way to a clearing giving Mack a clear view of the villa high up on the hillside, where he's soon to meet the top man. It's a single storey, white, very impressive luxury villa, only a few years old and probably built bespoke for the owner, to his own design. The glass-fronted windbreaker sits to the front of a balcony that stretches the whole width of the villa, which no doubt gives to a full panoramic view of the fantastic Indian Ocean.

The 4x4 loses the dirt track and powers onto a smooth, well-built, English parquet-style redbrick driveway that would accommodate ten of the 4x4s. Ally and Ennis get out taking their new courier a little way up the path and into the cool air-conditioned ground floor of the villa.

Wow, Mack thinks. *This room's easily forty foot wide and twenty foot deep.* Huge white quarry tiles line the floor, and huge glass doors that lead to a large terrace; wooden seat loungers furnish the solid oak rectangular low-level drinks table. A fully bespoke bang-up-to-date kitchen gleams from every angle, looking like it's never been used. A rectangular oak dining table with twelve high-backed leather chairs surrounding it separates the kitchen from the lounge area. A bundle of crisp one hundred dollar notes sits on it.

Further up the room, in the lounge area, four cream three-seater settees surround two large low-level square, wooden tables. A few tall plants stand near a very large plasma screen on the far wall. A media system sits just underneath it. *There's a few bob here... Crime does pay,* he thinks, while clocking the room's dimensions, furniture and hazards.

Little does Mack know, there will be the deaths of four people in that room ... within a short while.

A sweaty fat chap with a dodgy hairdo and wearing a white linen shirt, white shorts, and white sandals obnoxiously walks in through an adjoining door.

"You must be Mack!" he says, brashly making his way over to the three of them. Holding his hand out, he smirks. "I see you've been introduced to my bodyguards?"

This is said with a hint of sarcasm, as if Mack should feel intimidated by them – and him – or something.

"Yeah, we've met ... and here's your Kimber back," Mack says, also with a touch of sarcasm while looking at the Turks, then at the fat man as he reaches round his back retrieving the gun, handing it to Ali – handle first.

The fat man looks confused and a little concerned at this. Ennis explains what happened on the road to the meeting place. The fat man's eyebrows go up while looking impressed with Mack, and while moving the stack of dollar bills along the table a little says

"Maybe I should employ you, rather than these two, eh?"

"Maybe you should," Mack returns jokingly. As the fat man looks up at him.

"Okay, can I have the plates please," the fat man says, holding out his hand.

Mack hands him the rucksack.

Undoing the clasp he brings out the rolled-up linen. As it unravels, the shiny steel comes into view: silver-looking rectangular plates. The fat man holds them to the light. Mack can see them clearly now.

"Printing plates for the fifty euro note."

These plates, once on the printer, could pump out between sixty and eighty of these notes a minute. In addition, being the fifty-euro note, they could go all over Europe without even a question being asked. The fat man was going to do the five hundred Euro note but only gangsters play with those...and the last thing anyone wants to do is palm off dodgy notes to people who will kill you without even batting an eyelid. So the fifty it was.

"Yes, yes, yes," the fat man says slowly under his breath, while looking closely at them.

"Take them to the engraver" he brashly orders, passing them over to Ennis.

The plates were crudely put together elsewhere, but now they needed to be in the hands of one of the best engravers in the world, who just so happens to live in Thailand.

Turning back to Mack, he picks up the wad from the table and gives him $2000 in fifty-dollar notes.

"I trust your journey was okay?" he asks in a very-much-in-charge tone. "You came very well recommended and now I can see why." He says looking disappointingly at Ennis and Ali.

"In a couple of days I'll need you to take the plates to Chiang Mai for me for completion. Then, after a couple of days of being in the hands of the finisher, you take them back to Bangkok where the switch will be made back again for the polishing. You then get paid, and we part company," the fat man says.

"No problem," replies Mack.

"In the meantime, the beach here in Haad Rin is beautiful, and there's a full moon party tonight, which only happens once a month.

So why don't you stay and relax ... enjoy the tradition of the full moon we have here?"

"Yeah, sounds great, I'll see you soon." Mack makes his exit, saying goodbye to the Turks, following the way back down the track to the beach of Haad Rin further down.

Mack knows that when the switch has been made in Bangkok, he'll be a target for the hit-man. This is the most dangerous part of the operation. This is when Mack and the team cash in, or Mack checks out!

Chapter 15

Mack in wonderland

The bar's a little cooler than on the beach at Haad Rin. The ceiling fans turn at a speed that gives a good draught to sweaty shoulders. A cold Singha cools Mack's hand as he contemplates his moves over the next five days.

There are only three people in the bar, yet this is the famous Cactus Bar of the full moon party that he's heard so much about. As time goes by the bar slowly, but steadily, gets busier. The women are in abundance. Tall, thin, short, ugly, beautiful, English, German, Thai, lady-boys – all shapes sizes and colours. Mack looks out onto the beach. The music's started, and a sub-bass rocks the bar as a high-hat tinkers away further up the beach. *They all seem very jolly. A bit weird to be honest. Just seems they're all a bit over excited about just being here, rather than for the music and the festival to celebrate the full moon.*

He decides to go for a stroll, to see how things are working. The sand's now cooling as the day starts to disappear, the night gets hungrier for its feast of pick-pocketing and the drug-fuelled sex-craved all-nighter.

Feeling a bit peckish, he strolls into the peach bar where they serve food. An English waitress greets him with a hello. Mack says hello right back and orders the special omelette from the thirty or so omelette dishes advertised on the board above his head.

This bar could be anywhere in the world – typically Westernised to cater for the Western visitors. Mack thinks it's a shame that such a beautiful pocket of beach paradise can be ruined so easily by Westerners, and their drug-fuelled parties, however where there's money to be made... Let's face it, if it wasn't for the Westerners then there wouldn't be an income, and the beach would be dead.

The night pumps with bass lines. Walking along the shoreline after his food and beer, he finds all different types of music set ups – house, techno, trance, techno-trance, funk, soul – in fact anything that gets the inner soul moving.

A makeshift bar made up of a wallpapering table holds his wants for the evening. It stocks small buckets, like sand-castle buckets, but smaller, rounded. In them are 250ml bottles of whatever spirit he wants, and a mixer with straws. Mack buys the gin and tonic, pours the sealed bottle of gin in with the tonic and as much ice as will fit. Then he starts the walk along the busy, buzzing beach, contentedly supping away through the straws, soaking up the atmosphere.

A multi-coloured painted Thai chap with an extremely large lizard on his shoulder walks up to Mack, expecting him to take a picture for two hundred baht. Mack walks off. *Fucking weirdo.* Finding this funny, he starts to laugh out loud.. *Why the fuck would anyone want to walk around with a lizard on their shoulder?*

The lights and lasers were brilliant. A weird girl walking up to people and pulling stupid faces obviously did nothing for the people she was with, as they make plenty of space between her and themselves. He couldn't help but to start feeling the rhythm from each set that he passed, while supping away on his second bucket.

Large woven straw mats lie on the sand; areas of relaxation to sit down, chat, move on to another one are in abundance. People dress in multi-coloured nylon wrap-rounds; there are plenty of black people, and white people sporting Rasta style hair. Mack thinks it must be the 'done' thing not to wash your hair or something while in Thailand. Resting on a reed mat, comfortably watching the rest of the party jump and dance Mack notices that the partygoers seem to be strangely loved up, closing his eyes, he lets his head fall back and enjoys the moment.

A very large lizard is close by.

Mack's trying to ride his push bike to the ferry port in France. His body doesn't seem to want to do what it's told. In slow motion – which makes him put loads of effort in because he's going so slowly – he manages to push the pedals round. Arriving at the port with a sense of urgency, he finds he's on the wrong side of town for the ferry. He now has to peddle that unstable, hand-painted black 1960s push bike that takes so much effort around to the other side of town, to the other port.

When he arrives he's in the middle of a square in France. He doesn't know or understand where he is. It also becomes apparent that he's naked, absolutely starkers; but he's not cold, even though everyone else is fully clothed with coats on as if it's the middle of winter, and looking at him like he's a complete weirdo.

His clothes are under his arms, his push bike is leaning up against a bench right next to a bin.

What the fuck? Mack tries to put his clothes on. Every time he tries to put his leg through his jeans, he can't, because he's trying to put his leg through his shirt sleeve. *Eh?* Where are the shorts? *Fuck the shorts, I'll go commando.* But his socks are stuck in the shirt sleeve, so he can't get his jeans on. *For fuck's sake!*

A man walks up to Mack, he's wearing a technicoloured dream coat. Mack recognises him from the party. He doesn't know him, but the man seems to know Mack.

"What are you doing?" he asks with an inquiring expression. " C'mon, I'll take you home." The man says as if he knows Mack and knows what he`s like.

Mack goes with him, not knowing quite what else to do. He arrives home, still naked and carrying his clothes. He doesn't recognise his wife. She's a hard-looking woman with a *get on with life* attitude. His kids don't recognise him as a loving father; he's just the provider.

In fact, it turns out that he's a property developer, in France, and his partner in business is this bloke who he remembers talking to from the party at Haad Rin beach.

Mack's trying to tell his wife and kids, who are all in the kitchen, that he's not the horrible hard bastard that everyone thinks he is.

They just look at him, like its normal for Mack to walk around and do exactly as he pleases – naked. They don't understand. Mack looks at his wife.

"How long have we been living in France?" he asks.

"Two years," she replies, as if he's gone mad and should know how long they've lived there.

Mack can't remember even going to France, let alone living there and building a business. He must have amnesia or something. He can only remember being at the party ... two years ago?

"Someone must have spiked my drink, which in turn has caused amnesia" he tries to explain to everyone in the kitchen. They think he's finally flipped this time. He carries on trying to tell them that he's not this mad man they're all thinking he is right now, and that he can't remember anything about the last two years.

His wife explains that he did once go to a party similar to what he's talking about, and came back that night with a friend to tell all the family that they were moving to France because of a work deal.

Mack has been grumpy, moody, not paying any attention to his family, ever since.

Mack's wife doesn't look like his wife. She's pretty, well dressed with nice hair, which is short and highlighted. His youngest daughter is getting upset by his apparent loss of memory and starts to cry.

Mack lovingly picks her up, but she tries to push him away and go to her older sister, who has obviously dealt with all her pain and frustration, while dad has been an arsehole attending to the business rather than his family. She doesn't understand her *new* dad, and she doesn't trust him. This breaks Mack's heart.

Mack remembers when she used to come running into the bedroom at the crack of dawn, waking the whole house up. At first he had been angry to say the least, at being woken up at that time of the morning, which – being mid-summer – was at around five. He remembers not wanting to tell her off because she knew no better. So he invented a clock.

He went out and bought a large standard clock, then cut some red hour fans, and stuck them onto the clock. Now then, his daughter went to bed at eight o'clock; so the seven to eight o'clock was in yellow, and the rest of the clock-face was in red.

He taught her that if the little hand was in the red, she was to stay in bed; and when the red hand was in the yellow, it was time to be mellow.

After only a couple of sleeps she had learnt that when she woke up and the red hand was in the red, she stayed in bed. So as soon as the little hand went into the yellow, she could wake the house up. Mack had got a good sleep at last.

He remembers these times as good, but she wouldn't. She was only three years old. Mack starts to get angry because no one understands him; or rather, *he* doesn't understand what's going on.

"What the fuck has happened in the last two years!?" he shouts out loud, trying to make sense of it all.

Mack's mate comes in, the same chap who was at the party two years ago. Mack doesn't even know him, and yet he's his business partner. Not only that, but they've done well. They own two blocks of flats which they built themselves, and now they rent them out with a substantial income.

Mack realises they're rich; they live in a beautiful house and are set up for life. But he can't remember doing any of it. In fact, as far as he can remember, he's not even married. *But hey!* he thinks to himself as all of this is starting to sink in. *Things maybe aren't so bad after all. All I have to do is win the hearts and trust of my family back, and life will be great. Money, prospects, a loving family unit, what could be better?*

Mack grabs a wrist that's in a jeans back-pocket. He jumps up, folds the wrist-owner's arm under his armpit while pulling the wrist down hard. Crack! A Thai man runs off along the beach, mingling in with crowd, holding his wrist in pain. Mack knows it's broken.

He hears the sound of the bass speakers and people around him chatting, smiling, and laughing. *What the fuck?* He looks at his watch. Two hours have gone by. *Some fucking weird dream, that one.* Mack almost wishes it had been true.

Heading back to the bar where he earlier ate his omelette, and checking out the food and conversations around him, he overhears a conversation between a couple of party-goers;

"Have the special omelette. It's a magic mushroom omelette." *Well there you go,* he thinks. *That'll explain a lot.*

However, it still doesn't change the mixed emotions he has regarding his kids. The fact that he hardly sees them and that no woman will ever match up to what he expects from a wife, almost makes him wish the dream was real.

Mack makes his way to the town area to find a place to get a cab back to Had Sadet, retrieve his bike, ride back to Mai Haad, and get his head down ready for the journey ahead.

Chapter 16

The Journey to Chiang Mai

Day 6

The stifling heat of the hut's put liquid on the high priority list; Mack needs to rehydrate himself. Chucking on a T-shirt and flip-flops he makes his way over the hot walkway, passing the beautiful morning scenery to the reception area. Pulling open the fridge and grabbing a bottle of Singha, the cool waft hits him. *Wish I could sit in there for a while,* he thinks, while downing the bottle in one go.

The phone which dug a groove into his hip overnight now connects with his provider, buzzing silently. Pulling it from the Levi's pocket, he checks it while giving his stomach relief by releasing a huge burp. A message tells him to meet the Turk at Thong Sala tomorrow to pick up the goods. There, he can jump on the boat and make his way to Chiang Mai to where the 'finisher' will do his bit.

"Sawadeeka," says the small Thai lady behind the counter, looking at him with a little disgust as the smell from his burp still hangs in the air. Empty teeth cavities mixed with festering morning breath and beer don't make for a pleasant aroma.

"Morning. Can you organise a ticket to Chiang Mai for me for tomorrow?" Mack asks brashly, releasing another stinking burp into his hand.

"How you want to travel to Chiang Mai?" she says, now looking disappointed that his money will be leaving.

"Whatever's the cheapest, and I'll need the bike for one more day."

The price works out to 1,100 baht for the boat to the mainland, a coach to Bangkok, then a night train to Chiang Mai. Mack decides that today he will go snorkelling around the bay and island – the final wind down.

The accommodating deck chair has given him plenty of support over the last few days while he's been overlooking the bay, the sun calmly going down. As it does on his last night on the island; a feeling of sedation relaxes Mack to the full, remembering the afternoon's snorkelling and the thousands of sea slugs that littered the sandy bottom. He hates slugs, worms, snakes ... in fact, anything that looks or feels slimy. However, the colourful fish seemed to enjoy Mack being there, swimming close, and then darting off into the coloured coral reef as if asking for a game of chase. Mack knew that he'd enjoyed the swim because he could hear his own breathing through the snorkel that ran up by his ear. He had listened to the irregularity of his breath and the deep laughter that almost choked him on more than a few occasions.

Flicking the cigarette packet on the bottom with his thumb, a filter flicks up from the top. Sparking it up, he blows a long plume of relaxed smoke out into the calm warm air. Noticing the heat waves coming from the outline of the blood red sun, his toes move the sand around finding the cooler temperature of the sand deeper down. *Fucking beautiful.* The evening dullness eventually turns to night time black as the sound of the night creatures loudly orders him to his hammock to finish off the evening, with his own great company.

The morning brings an even sweatier day and thoughts of packing. Packing the rucksack as tight as he can and closing the door behind him, he knows the next few days won't be as relaxing as the last.

Mack checks out and pays for the bike. The Thais who run the establishment bundle his sack onto the back of the truck while he jumps on board, shouting thanks to the ladies who wave him goodbye. The taxi ride to Thong Sala costs nothing. Arriving at the small port the Turk's standing near the dock looking at the information board.

"Cheers mate, and thanks for everything," Mack says to Long as they shake hands goodbye. Long being the owner of the place he just stayed at in Mai Haad.

"Hello mate," he says to Ennis as he strolls up to the info board.

"Hello Mack, here's your stuff." Ennis replies, and hands him a well-wrapped and taped brown parcel. It feels heavy. "Are you on the next boat?" the Turk asks.

"Yup, then a coach to Bangkok, and a train to Chiang Mai."

"Okay, have a safe journey and thanks for the piece back," the Turk replies with a grin of respect. Mack smiles at him, giving a cheeky wink as the Turk walks off, looking at Mack over his shoulder. Safely nestling the cargo into the well packed rucksack, he's now settled in for the boat ride back to Surat Thani.

***

Mack's now travelled by boat to Surat Thani, then by coach to Bangkok, and now he's on the sleeper train to Chiang Mai.

To acquaint himself with the train he walks the whole length of it, then finds his seat number; forty-six. *These seats do well to accommodate the larger person, not seeming busy. Well, ho-hum, where's the beer carriage?*

The refreshment carriage is five carriages up and well equipped. The menu board advertises cooked breakfasts, dinners, and of course all other snacks and drinks. The carriage accommodates solid tables fixed to the floor, dressed with tablecloths and the usual silver restaurant cutlery. After browsing the menu for a split second, he orders the safe option, chicken and rice again with a bottle of coke. The acid in the coke will hopefully kill off any unwanted under-cooking.

The half-full carriage has the cosy surroundings and ambiance of any train on a long journey. Staring out of the window, the landscape's fantastic, barren, almost desert-like. It somehow reminds him of tranquillity, freedom, solitude and— Bang! The door smashes open.

Four Brits make their presence known as they shout their mouths off as if they're VIP. Sitting at a table, occupying two, they get their packs of cards out as they start their Brits on the piss ritual of guzzling booze, disrespecting the furnishings with legs draped on the tables and feet on the seats. No thought is given to other passengers. All this way from good old England, and even here they have to spread their plague of bad manners.

Typical. Loud, obnoxious and fucking annoying! Stupid pricks, he thinks, looking out of the window and trying not to be part of their idiocy. *Well, the sun's gone down, these fucking pricks are winding me up, and I want to get back to my seat to chill out for a while, before we get to Chiang Mai.*

Making his way out of the carriage, a brand new scene greets him. *What the? Where have all the seats gone? The whole train's turned into a bloody bunk bed! I don't even know which carriage I was in, let alone which bed. Great!*

After disturbing a few Thais and peering in between their curtains, a pretty Thai girl notices that he's a little oiled and confused as to where he is. Being able to speak English a little, she asks him what number he has. He shows her the number on his ticket, while having thoughts of him not finding his seat, and bunking down with her. She points to a top bunk further up the carriage. Saying thank you and half-staggering up the aisle, Mack's a little gutted she found it for him; still, nice thoughts of what he would have liked to happen give him something to think about when settling down.

He wearily pulls the curtain across. *Yep, this is the one.* Turning round to say thanks, he finds she's gone. The small oval shaped number, stamped in silver and riveted to the ceiling confirms he has the right place. Mack climbs up onto the bunk. *Nice: clean white sheets and a pillow.* He takes his shoes off, puts them against the rounded plastic carriage ceiling, and gets comfortable.

The carriage is quiet except for the sound of the train wheels rumbling over the steel tracks. Mack has time to relax and think a little. From the sound of the train he realises that it is travelling fast – very fast compared to the easy medium sound for the last five hours or so. The more he listens, the worse it gets, or so it seems.

Has the driver fallen asleep or something? I don't think we're supposed to be going this fast. The wheels keep coming off the tracks. When we hit a lump, there's a split second or so of silence, which means the wheels are no longer on the track, and if the wheels are not on the tracks for a split second or so while turning a corner, the train will derail, and we'll all be dead.... Great!"

Mack has visions of his daughter playing innocently, happily around him, laughing and cuddling him with her strong little arms round his neck, her little face pressed up to his, giving that unconditional love that all children do before they grow up, and get pumped full of aggression, greed, vanity, envy, pride ... and all the other crap that makes up the war-torn world. Thoughts of his little girl going through life without the knowledge that Mack has worked so hard to gather, isn't a good one. She wouldn't know the voice of the person that she is half of, one of the few people on this planet who would die for her at the drop of a hat, if need be.

Bollocks! I'm not ready to die, and certainly not in a speeding night train in fucking Thailand because of a fucking driver who's fallen asleep, for fuck's sake.

Mack's a control freak, and dying because of someone else's incompetence isn't on his agenda. He has two choices; one: go and make sure the driver isn't asleep...or two: put trust in the driver and calm down. Mack calms himself thinking that its probably the norm for this journey. As he does so, the train seems to slow down. Managing to relax enough, he drifts into the solitary realms of brain recuperation.

Day 7

A universal din of people starting their day brings Mack's mind, body and soul back to his cocooned slumber. Doors at each end open and close – the sounds of silence turning to ongoing themes. Mack's eyes open after his ears make out what's going on in the carriage. Opening the curtains, daylight floods in as the people around go about their business.

We must be nearly there. Mack pulls his trainers on and the curtains back fully. The thought of breakfast with a cup of tea summons him to the refreshment carriage. A bowl of cereal and a cuppa rinses the thick mucus from his stale mouth. Staring out of the carriage window and taking no notice of the landscape going past, the caffeine in the tea gets it all working again. A freshen-up in the toilets to wash away the last remaining residue from his slumber make the arrival to Chiang Mai acceptable.

The train slows to a trot. It travels at this speed for at least an hour. The passengers gather their belongings, ready for the departure. Mack's already standing by one of the doors, drawing on a burn, watching the morning landscape slowly pass by as he focuses on boulders and pits, he breathes through his nose to sample the fresh morning air, on every fourth breath.

They pull into Chiang Mai. Happy that the journey's finally over, Mack wanders out into the new and alien territory.

"Hello," he hears from behind him. Turning round, It's a cabby.

Mack smiles to himself and says, "Hello," right back, and carries on walking into town. He knows of a guest house called Grace's, recommended to him by Long. If he can buy a local map and find the guest house, all will be well.

Chapter 17

A soldier of freedom

By midday, Mack's soaking up the sights of Chiang Mai on the back of a Tuk-Tuk. It's not as busy as Bangkok, but at the same time it has the feel of a large town. The Tuk-Tuk man's showing him around by way of three wheels, in and around the area, getting him a little more acquainted with the surroundings before dropping him off at Grace's.

Grace's guest house stands bright and clean, situated down a pretty back street. The Tuk-Tuk stops outside the guest house, the sound of the two-stroke engine idles as the baht changes hands. A rather large black wrought-iron gate, with a smaller one adjacent to it welcomes Mack as he stands up on the side of the road.

Entering through the small entrance under the "Grace's" sign, he walks down a short path through a well-kept and pretty garden where the reception greets the tourist. Looking at the prices, Mack realises it's not cheap accommodation, considering it's not a hotel – 450 baht per night, even including breakfast seems a little steep, however, to convert it to Stirling, it would still be cheap in comparison, so happily pays for four nights and is shown to his room.

Quite nice as it goes, quality not quantity, he thinks to himself, looking around at the marble floors and en suite. *A comfortable-looking double bed, air con and a good view of next door's flower garden.* The walls have a white textured finish like the European's walls, and clean facilities. *Right then. Shit, shower, shave, shampoo – and maybe a shag later.*

Washed, changed and ready to hit the new town of Chiang Mai, he's ready to deal with whatever's on the agenda. An incoming message bleeps loudly from the nokia.

:Meet contact at the Kawila stadium tomorrow 16.00: *Fair enough ... now then ... where's the bar?*

A white corridor leads the way to marble stairs. The restaurant's to the right of the main entrance. Black-and-white pictures of the guest house and what could be the owner's family cover the wall. *Nice. It's good to see family values, and it smells of cleaning materials too.* Mack can see why Long recommended the guest house.

The pretty back street relates to somewhere like Australia, the same climate, well maintained, picturesque. Reaching the main drag, the famous city walls of Chiang Mai look almost impressive. However, Mack has to get his bearings and know where the stadium is. Walking just off Chang Moi road, he finds it. A sign on the gates shows the entrance to the stadium surrounded by a huge chicken-wire fence. It's closed. *Okay, at least I know where it is, that's the main thing. Oh! And bugger me ... it's smack bang next to a bar. How accommodating.*

Mack orders a Chang, again he doesn't get the frozen flannel treatment, or have a cool whirring fan pointed at him like in Bangkok. Being further north, Chiang Mai is a little cooler, and the people aren't as dark as down south. The bar seems to be a little more westernised. Beer pumps, shot glasses, and bar-type ornaments mingle in with a good selection of spirits, all covering the back bar. A fan hangs from the ceiling with wires dangling dangerously from the connector. However, it turns slowly without any worrying sparks leaping from it.

Three Thai chaps who display multi-coloured tattoos covering them from the neck down, play pool on blue baize table at the far left of the bar. Mack watches for a while as he drinks his beer. Western house music plays at an acceptable volume - not too loud.

Mack's got a whole evening on his hands to do how he pleases, so deciding to make this venue his home for the rest of the day and evening, he settles in. After more than a few bottles of the brew, and feeling fully relaxed, he's ready to introduce himself to the pool table, and make some new friends.

The pool playing Thais seem to be okay, and after clocking every table, chair, and drink, and reading the food menu five times over, and even noticing the fact that not all the toilets have paper, he decides to offer the Thais a game. Placing a coin on the side of the pool table, which leaves the universal sign that he wants to play the winner of the game being played, Mack returns to his seat.

The Thais go quiet for a second or two, looking at the money on the side. They look at each other; smiles slowly broaden across their faces. Mack likes this, when others make assumptions about him before knowing him, it gives him the upper hand straight away.

The word "*Farang*" seems to be repeatedly mentioned, greeted with nods and smiles from the homies. Mack waits for the game to end, which it does by way of one of the Thais knocking the balls in all pockets with his hand.

"Hello." The voice comes from that Thai. Mack watches as he slowly pulls a wad of notes from his pocket, giving a note to the other with loud words, handshakes and laughter.

The Thais retire to the bar area and sit at the stools without giving Mack a glance. Mack walks over to the table, puts his money in the slot, and pushes in the metal coin dispenser. The balls drop from their hopper, rumbling down the chute to gather at the bulkhead of the table's large opening. Finding the triangle on the floor he places it on the baize, careful to dust it off first.

The Thais' eyes bore into Mack as he sets the balls up in Western fashion, which he had noticed earlier was how they were setting them up. Choosing a cue from the blue baize, he heads back to his stool, then sits and waits for the winner of the last game to approach the table.

One of the Thai chaps moves to the table. Mack follows him. The Thai man pulls two hundred baht out of his pocket and puts it on the table.

"Okay?" he says, looking at Mack with a 'no messing about' expression.

Mack pulls out two hundred baht and plants it on top. "Okay," he says, with a 'That's fine with me' smile.

Things seem to be warming up already for Mack, and he hasn't even hit a ball yet. With the other cue in his hand, the Thai goes straight to the 'D' and plants the white ball inside it. Mack knows he's going straight for the break. However, they haven't flipped for it yet.

Mack moves close to him and gets out a coin.

"Okay," he says with the coin in view and ready to flip.

The Thai looks at him and smiles to his friends, as if to say, "Maybe this farang isn't as stupid as he looks?" and then points to the side he wants. Mack flips with the coin landing on the table; the Thai wins the toss, Mack gives him the nod to break.

Crack! The balls fill the table with moving colours as the Thai confidently circles the table while chalking his cue. A spot goes down, followed by another. By the time the Thai's finished his visit, he's only got two balls left. Mack puts up a fight and pots four of his stripes. The Thai returns to the table, only leaving the black for himself. Mack takes a swig from his bottle, checks all the angles by eye level, cues up and finishes his stripes.

The black's awkwardly on the cushion with no double available – a possible triple but too dodgy. He plays it safe, leaving the black on the other cushion and the white up the bulk end. The Thai looks at him, cues up and – whack! – the black's bouncing off all cushions and, plop, falls into the corner pocket. He calmly walks to the money and, without looking at Mack, conceitedly puts it in his pocket, then goes to the bar and carries on the conversation with his friends, this time looking serous.

Okay ... how about another game?

Mack gets out a two hundred baht note, and puts it on the table. The Thais at the bar stop talking and look at each other, grinning. The winning Thai walks to the table, looks at Mack and shows him four hundred baht. *So, he wants to up the stakes does he?* Mack puts another two hundred on the table, to make up four.

This time, Mack works hard winning the game – all square.

One of the other Thais lays a crisp five-hundred-baht note down, as if to ask if Mack's up for it. Mack matches it. He's loving this. To him, it's just a bit of fun; to the Thais, it's serious stuff, One thousand baht to them is a lot of money – a week's wages, by all accounts.

Mack flips, wins and breaks. The balls land nicely, with two stripes going down. After Mack's visit, only one stripe's left. The Thai, after his visit, has only one spot left. Mack clears the table and takes the money without giving his opponent a second glance, just like the Thai earlier.

The Thais have grown a little agitated, not happy, and the atmosphere's getting a little uncomfortable. Mack can tell the Thai wants his money back. *If he wants his money back, he's gonna have to win it back,* he thinks to himself defiantly.

The bar goes quiet with an atmosphere you could cut with a knife. The Thai walks over to the table, looking at Mack he lays another five hundred baht note down. Mack matches it, by laying his money on top. He loses the toss. The Thai breaks.

Shit break, mate. I've got this game in the bag; however, I don't want any trouble, and I don't need the money ... so I'll play to lose.

Mack's white bounces off the cushion after potting a ball and into the pocket. *Right, he's got two shots, all his balls are in good positions. He should clear up from here, which will chill him – and them – out a little.*

The Thai smiles, as if to think Mack's a dick. Not knowing that if Mack was at home he would have whipped their arses at this game all day long, and then if they'd got the hump he'd have wrapped the pool cues around their heads for good measure...However, he's not at home, and he doesn't need any grief right now. The Thai cleans the table of his colours. *Good.*

He then hits the black straight into the side pocket. The only trouble is, he's hit it too hard, so the white carries on slowly down the table...and disappears down the corner pocket. *Wanker! Anyone could see that if he hit that too hard it would be an in- and- off.*

The Thai at the bar starts shouting at his mate, who's looking in disbelief at the table, then the money on the side. Mack casually walks up, takes the money, and sits down without making any eye contact.

An argument starts between all three of them. *If I leave now, they'll probably follow me to get their money back, and then I'll have to do the silly pricks.*

Mack needs another way of dealing with this situation. Walking over to the Thais, he puts fifteen hundred baht on the bar. Aggressively they gesture for him to put the money away. Mack realises that as much as want their money back, they won't 'take' it back without winning it. If there's one thing the Thais honer its a fair play. However, they now think Mack's a hustler and don't want to take the chance of losing any more. *I wasn't going to 'give' it back anyway you stupid pricks!* Mack thinks to himself.

"You do tattoo?" Mack asks, pointing at their tattoos.

"Yeh," replies the Thai man with the most tattoos, looking angry, and a little confused as to the question.

"Okay, you tattoo me," he says and slides the fifteen hundred baht along the bar towards him.

"AH!" exclaims one of his friends. The Thais are talking fast, the anger moves to relief. They're going to get their money back, and in return give Mack a cheap tattoo in its place.

Taking the money, they buy Mack a beer. They're all trying to ask him what tattoo he wants. Fortunately, the bar maid speaks a little English, and she's able to translate roughly what's going on to all involved. Mack asks them what they think he should have in Thai writing. They all ponder, after talking a while between them, they relay it to the barmaid. The barmaid then says to Mack what they think he should have. They have suggested, "This man is a soldier of freedom", *how nice of them to say so*, to go down the left side of his torso.

Mack agrees and tells them to write it on a piece of paper. With the paper in his hand, he goes to another bar and asks if anyone can translate into English what is says. It's confirmed. Mack goes back to the bar.

"Okay," he says brashly with a 'we're now all on the same level' attitude. The Thais are happy, finishing their drinks; they beckon him to go with them.

Arriving at a very small lock-up down a side street, they unlock the padlock and slide open the metal corrugated door. Inside, the walls are covered with pictures of tattoos completed from wall to ceiling. There's a padded adjustable dentist's chair, with a wooden stool next to it. The Thai gestures Mack to lie down and take his top off. Putting on a pair of gloves, he gets things organised, then turns round with a traditional bamboo tattooing tool, inking the point up, he starts tapping on the wood, the wood holding the spike, taps into Mack.

Chapter 18

A Butterfly bites

Day 8

Mack wakes, knowing that he has to be somewhere today. A pain on his side wakes him fully. *Shit! I forgot about that!* Slowly running his hand over the taped up tattoo – inked last night while he was in a drunken stupor – brings it home. The visions of the crowd that gathered around as the pain sweated from the pores of his face gives him the realisation that the words on his side will be there forever. "This man is a soldier of freedom."

He also remembers going to another bar afterwards and chatting to a Thai lady who spoke broken English. *I think I'm supposed to be meeting her later today ... somewhere? Okay, let's have a look at this tattoo then.* Mack slowly pulls the tape and dressing off. *Okay ... it's not too bad. In fact, I quite like it.*

He takes off his shorts and turns the shower to warm. Walking under the warm water on the cold floor, he runs his fingers over the new addition. *Its bumpy, but it doesn't hurt. I'm not supposed to get this wet, but how do I do that in a shower?* He washes thoroughly, changes and then gets down to the organising of today's meeting. A rumble in his stomach reminds him that he needs fuel. Passing the reception on the way out, he asks if they can do him an omelette. They can. *Not a special one this time though, eh?*

Mack makes his way down the same side street that he walked down yesterday. He walks past the tattoo shack, pokes his head in and says hello. The Thais greet him like he's an old friend, offering to fill in the letters that were inked last night. Mack declines, as his hunger needs attending to.

A small pizzeria shows him the delights that would satisfy the feeling of hunger. He orders the pepperoni, a growl from within agreeing with his choice. While it's being cooked, he heads off to find an English paper, The *Daily Express*.

The only paper that says it how it is, Mack thinks.

Reading the paper, eating the pizza and drinking a Chang, Mack feels very much at home and in touch. Time's getting on for three-ish, and remembering the lady from last night, it just so turns out that he's meeting her at the same place where the switch will be occurring later, the Kawila stadium.

The Kawila stadium's gates are open this time, but the place is empty. However, there are at least ten, maybe twelve make-shift bars surrounding the ring. *Nice, at least I can wait in comfort.* Mack's attention's immediately drawn towards an area in the corner of the stadium. Looking over, he sees there's some sort of commotion as loud music erupts. He jumps, a little startled by the noise. It's coming from the speakers that perch precariously in each corner of the arena.

Even he's a little surprised to see what's exiting from what looks like dressing room doors. A woman, wearing the most over-the-top get-up he's ever seen ... and he's seen a few. *What!!! What is going on?* he thinks in major surprise.

The woman's wearing a red and gold ball gown, so big that it spreads about three-square metres around the base of her feet. She glides out of the changing rooms, glinting brightly, showing off boldly and making everything around her pale into insignificance. The piece is so well fitting she looks like a cross between Queen Victoria and Lilly Savage. The headpiece fanning out to about four times the height and width of her head, is glitzy, no messing around. The woman's make-up's well over the top to say the least. She looks like something out of a circus; however, you can tell she's proud of what she's wearing because of her smile, a smile to suppress any negativity around her. *Jeepers!*

Mack sits at a barstool, still trying to comprehend what's happening with amazement and not taking his eyes off the women coming from the room. He orders a Chang. The barmaid puts it in his hand. Noticing his amazement she starts giggling. Mack looks at her completely bemused.

"What's this?" he asks, looking at her in wonder.

"It's the lady-boy parade," she coyly says in good English. "They're practising for the parade next week."

"Oh! They're not women?"

"Yes ... they are women," she replies sternly. "They are lady-boys!"

He doesn't need any more explanation, he gets the picture. "Okay," he replies slowly, and focuses on his beer.

Time's getting on, and in all fairness Mack doesn't feel at all comfortable watching a load of lady-boys prancing around. He feels he's in the wrong place at the wrong time. The arena doesn't resemble the stadium in Bangkok at all. No chicken wire, no atmosphere, no benches – only two rows of seats with the walls almost prefab and the roof made of corrugated metal, with a few square clear sheets of Perspex letting in the daylight. In fact, if it wasn't for the warriors' ring, the venue wouldn't resemble a place of battle at all, more like a glorified collection of bars to accommodate a place for wrong 'uns.

The rucksack sits firmly sandwiched between his feet as he sits on the stool, looking around at his new surroundings. All the bars are empty of punters and staff. Any staff that are there seem to have their own areas to work in; however, when someone walks up to the bar anyone who's near walks behind the bar and serves the punter. A strange set up by all accounts.

A couple of the makeshift bars have pool tables, and even a space-invader type game can be seen at one of them, sitting lonely on the stone floor. Mack turns to look at the bar he's sitting at; not very well stocked, mainly bottles of Chang and Singha in two tall fridges. A picture of a butterfly is stuck to each of the fridges. *I wonder what they mean?*

A well-dressed Thai man plonks himself down on a stool next to Mack. He's wearing a well made grey flannel suit, with a white open shirt, and expensive leather shoes. Mack looks down: parked next to his rucksack is an identical one to his. The Thai orders a beer, drinks it and leaves. Mack looks down again: his rucksack's still there. *Well, that's what I call a switch, even I didn't notice that.*

Still impressed by the pure swiftness and no-hassle switch that just took place, he doesn't see a Thai girl walk the whole circumference of the stadium, spot him and make her way round to sit on a stool next to him, at the bar.

"Hello," she says in a cute voice, with the look of remembrance on her face.

"Oh. Hello," replies Mack, realising it's the same girl from the night before – the one he met after his tattoo encounter.

"How you doing? Do you want a drink?" Mack asks loudly, over the music.

"I'll have what you're having. The same as you," she replies loudly.

Mack orders up two Chang's. *My luck could be in tonight. The Chang's seven percent, so a couple of these should relax her enough.* They chink bottles, both taking large swigs.

Mack knows that the Thais are only after a free night, but he could also get a free night here too. He studies her facial features for a second; *green eyes. I've never seen a Thai girl with green eyes. Very pretty, nice tits – big, again out of character for a Thai. Hair straight, shoulder length. About a size-eight figure and five-foot tall. Perfect. I want to get this one into bed already. I'll not make the conversation, she can. That way any sexual instigations will be down to her, and I won't get collared by the confusion of a monetary transaction!*

"How long are you in Chaing Mai for?" she asks.

"Just a few days."

"Have you been anywhere else in Thailand, or is this your first stop?" she asks again.

"I came up from Bangkok to do the elephant riding," Mack replies.

"Oh, I've always wanted to do that" she says almost convincingly. "Are you travelling with anyone else?"

"Nope, just enjoying Thailand on my own," Mack replies, still not getting it.

This is how the conversation goes; small talk. The conversation progresses, but not as Mack would like it. *She wants to know the ins and outs of a ducks arse don't she?* Mack has to be careful so as not to give any info away, no matter how drunk he gets.

The phone vibrates in his pocket. *Another message.* Digging it out, he reads : Cargo ready 1 week, will contact:

Mack immediately hits hard the realisation that this isn't right, a sinking feeling in his gut sets in.

Shit! This ain't supposed to be how it is. I'm supposed to take this back to Bangkok in two or three days, the switch has already been made, so what's this all about? Something ain't right.

Mack now knows there's a problem; *could it be with communication on their side, has the link that did the switch only twenty minutes ago not told them he has the cargo? Everyone has a part to play, which includes the finisher. They get two days to do their stuff. Things have to go like clockwork otherwise it puts the whole deal out of sync. And when things go out of sync, people get nervous; and when people get nervous, all hell can break loose. Not only that, this Thai bird is asking a little too many questions for my liking. There's no way this bird, who I randomly bumped into last night, in a random bar, is a plant ... is there?*

Mack's state of mind is becoming incoherent. The last few seconds have knocked him sideways. The Thai lady, as much as he wants to shag her brains out, is being a little too inquisitive, and what with the message and vibe he's picking up from ... from somewhere ... he decides that the booze is starting to hamper him and his thoughts. *If things are going to get a little hairy, I need to have my faculties about me.*

The Chang's not working for him, it's not relaxing Mack or making things mellow, infact quite the opposite. He feels slow, off balance, it's working against him now. Paranoia's creeping in, which is a safety mechanism, but a bad state of mind to be in. Mack needs to go, get out of this situation, get his shit together.

Mack's finishing his bottle and putting the rucksack on his back when another suited Thai man sits next to him just as he's about to leave, and another sits next to the girl. *Out of all the empty bars in here, they sit next to us? No point worrying, just turn and go ... deal with it!*

Putting the bottle down, he cheerfully says cheerio to the girl, swivels on the stool, plants his feet on the floor, and starts to walk out. A shout comes from across the stadium, which is now quiet and empty of lady-boys, so echoes uncomfortably.

"Hello," a voice says from behind him.

Mack turns to see the suit who says, "You come with us," trying to grab Mack by the arm.

Mack does a full turn on his heel while slamming the arm away with his hand to break the grip. Another suit's quickly walking over. Mack doesn't think; he starts to run the opposite way round the ring.

A man with a pool cue in his hand walks towards Mack, eyes fixed. Now Mack knows he's in trouble, and activates escape mode. Grabbing the nearest chrome bar stool, he holds the seat up to his chest charging the Thai with it. The four feet of the stool jam into the Thais' upper body knocking him clean off his feet, which in turn smashes the cue in two as it lands underneath his aggressor on the hard stone floor, with a cracking sound.

Mack hurdles him discarding the stool, aiming towards the other exit. The other suit's cut his exit off. *No probs, I'll go through him.* Running straight towards the suit, two Thai policemen appear from the open exit. *Shit! Okay ... they can go too then!*

As Mack reaches the suit, all in one motion he leans into him with both arms out, left arm over the top of his right, slightly bent at the elbow, palm up, wrist forward, right arm moving forward, palm down, wrist forward. Slamming his left foot down to the floor as he stops dead, forcing his whole bodyweight behind the strike but no follow through. The momentous force transfers from Mack's torso, through his arms and wrists...and the 'Chi' is released... straight into the suit on impact, smashing into the upper chest and stomach. *An impact strike to take out the hardest man on the planet.* The suit's body absorbs the impact for a split second, then it kicks in – the shock wave hits. The man's chest cavity is forced into a flying backwards spasm with all internal organs rupturing into a mess, his chin slamming down onto his chest as his head is left behind in the flying backwards motion. The rest of jelly like body follows, legs and feet flying after him like a rag doll, shoulders slamming into the policemen behind, taking them out too, like the force of a battering ram, they go down in a heap of pain.

An arm goes round Mack's neck from behind. Focusing on another strike, again he finds the target stamping down with his heel onto the aggressors foot, while at the same time dropping his bodyweight, the aggressors grip's is instinctively released. Turning, he sees a Thai bloke in a T-shirt hopping around, with the sharp end of an elbow straight down onto the crown of his head, the Thai drops to the floor like a sack of potatoes.

Running towards another exit, the man with the cue is up and about again, now with half a cue in each hand. *Fair enough, but you should have stayed where I put you ... this time you go down for good.*

Mack dodges to the left as the wood tries to connect with his head blocking it with his right arm, he slides his hand down the wood firmly grabbing the half cue while snap-kicking the Thai in the groin, knowing that with a kick to the groin, the neck extends so as to expose a soft and deadly target. Releasing the half cue from his attackers grip, and in a circular motion he slaps it straight into the Thai's outstretched throat. Mack knows the Thai won't be getting up from this one, his throat will swell from the blow, he will suffocate and die by way of a severely swollen Adam's apple... unless he receives immediate attention.

One more to go, he thinks as he sees another obstacle by way of a man between himself and the way out of this scenario. A spinning back kick sends this obstacle into a group of stools like a bowling ball into its pins, smashing them in all directions, leaving the man in an entangled heap on the floor with a stool leg embedded into the dip his back.

Mack's out the stadium and sprinting down the road, overtaking the traffic, eyes focused on the end of the road, a long way ahead.

Leaving the carnage and sounds of sirens – which he hadn't heard before behind him he turns down many side streets to lose anyone who might have been able to keep up.

Realising he's now somewhere back to reality and in a busy street, he looks and feels out of place. By breathing heavily he's drawing attention to himself; everyone else is calm, happy, chatting, drinking, eating, and walking, he's sweating badly. Finding homage within steam coming from the stalls on the streets give him cover. He needs to blend in, lower his adrenaline, at least *look* like he's not in trouble.

Walking, his mind racing, he has to quickly put all this into perspective.

Why were the police there? Who were the suits? Who's got the plates? What the fuck has just happened? Are the plates in the hands of the police, or in the hands of the fat man's people? If they're in the hands of the police, then the fat man is gonna want me bumped off early and I won't know where. However, if they're in the hands of the fat man, then all should be well.

He needs to text the fat man, to see if the plates are in *his* circulation. If not, then a new plan will have to be put in place, because Mack will be a target sooner than they thought. All the surveillance and cover is in Bangkok ... not Chang Mai.

Finding a small out of the way restaurant, the calmness starts to settle in. Ordering a coke Mack realises he needs sugar, not booze, no more booze!

Taking the rucksack off, unzipping the top and looking in, Mack sees three stones taped together for weight. *Okay, someone's got the plates then.* Finding his phone, he texts to the number he received earlier. "Are the plates in your possession?"

He waits.

A message comes back from the fat man's people. :No. There was a fight. The exchange didn't take place. Have you still got the plates?:

Mack now knows that this means the plates are in the hands of someone else, maybe the police, judging by what happened back there. *Or the fat man's got the plates, and he's trying to stitch me up. This is probably not the case, as he wouldn't want me in the hands of the police and he wouldn't have the plates. Unless the police are crooked and working for the fatman. Or is someone else is trying to stitch me up? – someone on the inside, someone who's working for the police.*

Either way, he's now on the run, on his own, and in a city where he shouldn't be with no cover and no plan ... just how he likes it.

Chapter 19

Back to basics

Mack needs communication, a new phone, or at least a new sim card. A phone and a new sim card would be better as he needs to receive info from the 'ring', and have communication to his team. However, he has to be careful; for all he knows the sim card he has may well be on fat man's radar. If that's the case then he can't receive anything without giving away his position, or infact his intentions. Mack has nowhere to go. He doesn't want to go to the guest house, it may be under surveillance, and he can't be on the streets, it's too dangerous. Contacting the team is a must, they now need to know how things have changed.

The carbonated glass of coke manages to do the job of bringing his mind back to its senses; a sugary input brings awareness that his heart rate's returning to a normal beat, his adrenaline slowing brings on the conscious throbbing pain from where he was caught with some earlier blows. The lump on his arm where he blocked the cue swells, but if nothing's broken, then it'll be fine. Mack decides it's time to move on. Cautiously he leaves the bar making tracks into the street, blending in like a tourist casually crossing the narrow way...no commotion, no one shouting, no one chasing. *'Good; all seems well.'* But he now has the phone to deal with.

Mack spots a tech shop a few hundred yards up, and after spending ten minutes in there, he has a new unlocked phone with an unlocked sim card. The next move is to contact the team back home. He dials...

"Hello" comes the answer.
"Sticky" Mack says, and waits for the reply.
"Will contact in ten." The line goes dead.

Mack knows with a new number the team will have to check and secure the line before any communication can commence. Not only that; the password 'Sticky' has enough weight on its own to bring concern to the team.

Mack has three passwords. **Glue** means all is well. **Sticky** things have gone wrong, and **unstuck**...when this is said all communication goes down and a reconnoitre is activated, just so long as they know his location.

Mack chooses another cafe. He has to keep on the move, even if it's only a few shops at a time. The phone vibrates on his thigh. Reaching for the vibrating piece he slides it from the left pocket, looking at the screen. It's the team.

"Sticky" he says again as he puts it to his ear while still looking around for any shenanigans.
"The line is secure. Update, Mack" the voice commands.
"The switch was made in the Kawila stadium, the police were present and I'm sure special branch was too, It went sour."
"Is the target in receipt of the merchandise?" the voice proceeds to ask.
"I spoke to him an hour ago and he denies he has the merchandise."
"Leave it with us. You'll be contacted within the next 24 hours."
"Understood" Mack replies. The line goes dead. He puts the phone back in his pocket.

Mack needs food and a place to stay; somewhere cheap and inconspicuous. Checking his watch he sees that time's getting on. Ordering fried rice with chicken it comes out a steaming, the rice is sticky and the chicken moist. Watching the door with every mouthful Mack has to think of his next move, he knows the Thai police are as corrupt as any underworld organisation, and these people he doesn't want to be captured by, they're bad people.

Deciding to take his chances with a small hostel just up the street, the gut feeling he has is that things are reasonably safe for him there, for the short term anyway. Mack needs to change his appearance; different clothes and a hat of some description are top on the shopping list.

Leaving the bar, he approaches a shop that sells just about anything and everything. His peripheral vision's doing overtime while his ears are trained for any sudden noises, this brings back memories for Mack of good and bad times, Mack feels alive again.

Picking a grey cap from a hanger with the price of 100 baht inked onto a clipped-on piece of cardboard, a T-shirt and jeans and quickly checking around to see what most other Thai men are wearing, they're mostly dressed this way, so he should blend in just fine. Not looking like too much of a 'Farang' is the name of the game. Paying the lady he heads off towards the Hostel sign a little farther up.

At the old oak front table of the extremely basic guest house's entrance sits an old man,
"How much for four nights?" Mack asks, doing his best to be polite.
Smoke from the old man's clay pipe wafts into his darkly tanned wrinkled face. He slides a price list across the table like he's got all day, and backpackers are a bit of a pain, he doesn't even look up from his pebble shaped goldfish bowl glasses, or the falling apart book he's reading.

The hand written price list states 130 baht per night, and at 67 baht to the pound that makes for a room that's under two quid a night. Mind you...it is just a room...nothing else. Mack counts out 500 Baht sliding the price list back with the worn paper money on it waiting for some sort of reaction. Another plume of smock engulfs the old man's face as he takes the money, slowly and without looking, he roots around in an old metal safe box, finds a key and replaces the change with the key on the table, then points to the stairs, then checks Mack out through the top of his glasses.

Taking the key, Mack glances a thank you while making his way up the rickety steps and onto what feels like a bamboo walkway. Now the sun had set, and the lighting being one low wattage bulb for the whole corridor, trying to find his room number isn't easy. An old internal wooden door, like the ones you find in old 1930s houses doesn't have a light coming from its outline. Mack has to get his eye right up to it to make out the number. The number 14 becomes visible. The padlock opens easily, obviously well used. The door opens outwards with the dim light from the corridor illuminating the room, just enough for Mack to see an old bedside table made of what looks like oak, again, dating from around the 1930s, an old metal framed double bed with a well made mattress and a ceiling fan. Locating the light switch he flicks it down...no power.

"Great, no power means no fan, and no fan means a sweaty heavily interrupted sleep ahead. Still, I only need it for the night"

Mack changes into his new clothes, even though it would probably be better to sweat all night in his old ones, the thought of being interrupted by the police during the night, gives a need for a different ID. Rolling up the old ones, he puts them in a plastic bag, and under the bed. The springy bed gives comfort to aching muscles as he stares at the silhouette of the still ceiling fan, the days and future occurrences churning in his mind. The warm bamboo walls surround him while his ears listen out for anything out of the ordinary. Tomorrow he'll dump the old clothes, contact his team... and receive new orders.

His mind starts to relax, then his muscles, then his eyes.

***

Chapter 20

Clever Girl (Part 2)

Saturday night had arrived. Ted makes a couple of phone calls to order the coke. He doesn't feel right about the forthcoming night, however, they want his company and they need the coke, anyway seeing some of his old buddies would make a welcome change.

Driving round to Trudy's house with the posh and a crate of beer nestling on the back seat, he's ready, or at least he thinks he is.
 Balancing the slab of beer on his right arm, and with his free hand,
"Ding dong." The small single button returns to its untouched state.
A shadow immediately appears through the glass-paned front door.
It opens. Trudy's standing there, she's dressed up to the nines in moody clobber. (Mutton dressed as lamb.)
" Hey Ted," shouts Tony as Ted walks through the door and into the lounge.
"How are ya?"
"Yeah, I'm fine" he replies, giving Trudy a kiss on the cheek, walking in to the familiar surroundings and sitting down on the couch, which is the only place left to sit...right next to Bindi. Ted takes a few seconds to look at Bindi, while thinking how tasty she is.
"Hi Bindi." Ted says with a genuine smile. With a genuine smile she replies,
"Hi Ted, nice to see you again."
"And you" he replies with a bigger smile.

Ted's seat is nearest to the window, which leaves Bindi on his left, with Trudy and her husband to the left of Bindi, who sits on the couch. Trudy's looking at Ted with an 'I know something you don't' look.
Ted picks up on this and starts to think maybe this isn't as clean cut as he'd thought, however he brushes this idea aside as a mischievous look, knowing that drugs are on the menu so that's what it is.

Beers are offered around. Trudy doesn't have one, she's got her own cheap white wine from the crappy overrated Sainsbury's. She likes the cheap stuff..., which fits with her just fine.

The centre of the room has a large rug over a well carpeted floor, and the table's been moved out of the room, either that or they've got rid of it.

Looking at the open area on the carpet, Ted looks thinking it all seems a little stagey, but again overlooks the signs.

"Did you get the posh?" Trudy pipes up, eyes wide with anticipation.

"I got a Henry." Ted replies contentedly looking around for approval. (Henry the eighth, an eighth of an ounce, in weight)

She's secretly over the moon, not because she wants the drugs, but because once Ted's coked up she'll turn the whole conversation to sexual innuendos, and knows how the coke will play its part in getting the loins stirring, which in turn will run its course and ruin Ted and Helen's relationship.   (Yeah!..I have the power) goes through her power hungry mind... again)

"Excellent!" Tony replies as he does a little dance with his arms in excitement.

"So if you all want to chip in forty quid that will cover it" says Ted looking at everyone.

Trudy goes to the kitchen and comes back with some money. She leans in, and smiling sarcastically at him says

"Here you are Ted." She thrusts eighty pounds into his hand. Bindi roots around in her handbag and gives him forty pounds. Ted gets up and says he's going to divide the posh up in the kitchen.

"Hold on," says Tony, while flicking his eyebrows up and down at Ted,

"Use this." He then produces a good-sized mirror from down beside the couch, that he obviously put there for that reason.

"Nice" Ted exclaims while smiling, and empties the contents of the bag onto the mirror, which is now sitting level and ready to go on his lap.

Ted takes a NatWest debit card from his leather wallet, and starts to divide the powder into four even sections.

"Don't worry about all that, just get some lines together and we'll divide it up later" says Tony.
"Okay, whatever you say dude."

Portioning off a small amount from the main bulk, he proceeds to chop the posh into a finer powder. Ted's enjoying having something to do to be fair, it's taking his mind off his girlfriend Helen. He was thinking of her earlier, but when he saw Bindi, the thought of what he'd like to do with Bindi's naked body and big tits flooded his mind, consequently overpowering everything else, including his girlfriend...Helen.

A compilation of dance floor club sounds spin on the midi-hi fi. Ted 's thinking the tunes are plastic, commercial crap as he cuts the posh, remembering the score earlier.

After making his phone call to the only dealer he still knew, he made his way to the dealer's flat. Parking up, he walked to the buzzer and pushing hard on the square metal knob, he heard it cheaply buzz.
"Hello" a voice came through.
"Hello mate, it's Ted"
"Yeah mate, come up" the voice replied and the door latch buzzed, allowing him in.

Ted pushed the door and walked up four flights of stairs where bloke had his front door open, sporting a grin of the local Cheshire cat, knowing he was up for a good sale.
Following bloke through the front door and into the flat, then into the lounge, an old multicoloured carpet and a fake log fire came into view, one of those gas fires that heat up the back plates.
The main lights were on very bright, it must have been at least a 120 watt bulb or something. Some sort of weird and funky fern wallpaper that went out of fashion in the seventies covered the walls. This was the nineties and it hadn't come back into fashion yet.
In front of the 1980s three piece suite there was a 1960s wooden table, polished. On it was about five ounces of speed, next to that a big box of baking powder.
"Now then, I wonder why he had baking powder next to the speed?:Answer: He's been cutting the speed with the powder. Now that's rather silly considering when he got the speed it was already

cut to fuck anyway!" Ted had wondered just how much he had cut that shit...probably about 50/50... *'Tut tut... the bloke won't have many punters after that batch then will he? Silly prick!'*

So of course, now Ted's hoping the posh hasn't been cut too, especially as it was all bagged up and not weighed in front of him when he picked it up. Still, too late now, he should have dealt with that earlier.

Rooting around in his jacket pocket, he pulls out a CD, 'Leftism, by Leftfield'.
"There you go mate," he says to Tony. "Chuck this on; I think you'll like it" he says, leaning over and passing him the CD.
Tony looks around the room for approval of Ted's request.
"Nice, good tunes" Tony remarks.
"Yeah, good as gold, this album" Ted says without looking up.
So now Ted has four nicely cut lines of posh, all lined up and ready for lift off.
"Who wants to go first?"
"No, go on Ted" replies Tony, gesturing for Ted to go first.

Ted rolls up a score nice and tight, holds it with his right hand, closes off his left nostril, and gets himself into position. He puts the end of the score up his right nostril, and, while running the other end of the score along the line, snorts it. The line disappears up his nose as if by magic. Holding his head up high with the score still up his nostril, he breathes out of his mouth so any residue doesn't get blown out from inside the rolled up note. Tapping it on the mirror, a small amount of the coke sits there; he finishes this by picking it up with a wet finger, and rubbing it on his gums...like they do on the TV.

Looking down his nose he smiles approvingly at Tony. He in response nods his head while also smiling approvingly back. Ted passes the mirror to his left to Bindi. Bindi picks up the score and repeats the process, then passes it to Trudy.

The back of Ted's nasal area where it joins to the throat has disappeared, or that's what it feels like. This indicates that the posh should be good. *"You can't find many things off the shelf to duplicate that effect?"* he thinks.

Confidently looking around for approval of his shopping, he gets it.
"Where did you get this?" Tony asks.
"I got it from bloke" Ted replies, still a little unconvinced.
"Oh yeah!" Trudy comes back with eyes wide while starting to feel the effects.
"Some of his stuff can be shit though, can't it?" she says, while sounding like she's got a cold. This is what Ted was worrying about.

"Well, while I was round there," Ted starts, "he was knocking his speed down at least 50 % with cat's piss." (The term used for baking powder that smells like cat's urine.)
"Rude fucker!" Trudy remarks. "The last time I saw the bloke, he was chatting up some ugly tart at the bar in the lost soul, and she was fucking manky!" she says, laughing through a screwed up expression.
"He's a dirty fucker though, ain't he?" Tony replies with another screwed up expression.
"I went round there about six months ago to score, and he came to the door in a dressing gown. He was banging some weird bird from lazy town."
Tony starts laughing. "He told me he managed to get nearly half a pint of cum in a glass from her, as she was a squirter."
Ted laughs loudly and shouts, "Dirty fucker!"

Trudy can't believe her luck; the conversation's already turned the way she wanted it to go and she didn't even have to initiate it.
Knowing how to take advantage of this conversation, she says
"I don't know anyone that squirts when they cum," then scans the faces in the room for a follow up.
"Neither do I." Ted remarks, falling right into it.
"I've been with a few noisy ones in my time...but not a squirter"
"I love coming" Bindi says in a deeper tone, whispering it to herself with a very cheeky grin.

Trudy starts laughing with delight, knowing it couldn't be going better.
"Fucking hell!" Ted thinks, *"I don't know if I can handle being in the same room as Bindi, coked up, and her talking about orgasms without me wanting to try and shag her brains out."*

The room concludes that orgasms are good news, and most definitely take up a lot of boredom while looking for one, two, or even three. Ted thinks that Bindi's up for a little hanky panky tonight, and she's looking extremely fuckable; the posh is doing its job, which is bang on cue.

Ted's mood makes him chatty. On top of that, with all the chit chat about women's orgasms, he's feeling horny too.
There's nothing wrong with a bit of banter, but before he can begin Trudy starts,
"What part of a woman's body turns you on the most then, Ted?"
"Fucking hell! he thinks again, *"Trudy's getting fruity, ain't she? Still...a good question."* he doesn't have to think hard for the answer though

"A great pair of tits" he replies, happily knowing that Bindi has a massive pair. "I like them firm, rounded and smooth, with big nipples" he says, knowing how Bindi's tits are exactly that. (He heard it through the grapevine from someone who was shagging her.)

"What do you think of my tits then, Ted?" she asks in a provocative manner, looking him straight in the eye.

This really is the turning point for the whole evening. If Ted plays it down, there will be no problem. However, Trudy's already set the stage, and the narcotics to guarantee it will go the way she predicts.

"I don't know, I've never seen them, however from the outline they look pretty good." Ted's being polite, and he's starting to feel like this shouldn't be happening. Helen's face looms in his conscious thoughts, so he decides to take a little breather and move the conversation on.
"So what part of a man's anatomy do you like then?" he asks back at her.
"I like a good looking cock" she replies, looking Ted straight in the eye.
Again, Ted could get out of this by saying he's got an ugly cock and move on to music, but again, goes with the flow.

"And has your husband got a good looking cock?" he asks, moving it away from himself.

"Yes" she replies with a smile. "Go on, get it out!" she demands to Tony.

Ted and Bindi laugh loudly while Tony looks a little shocked, but at the same time he shrugs his shoulders and seems okay with it.

(Now then, if you're on cocaine, for a man the penis tends to turn into something resembling an acorn, so it's not a very flattering sight to say the least, certainly not something to boast about.)

Tony gets up, stands in the middle of the room and starts to undo his trousers, making Bindi squeal with delight. He drops his cacks and gets his knob out... Bindi immediately bursts out laughing while Tony looks a little embarrassed. The cocaine is definitely doing its job; Ted knows he's going to be the same.

"That's a good looking penis you got there bruv." Ted remarks.
"Thanks Ted" he says as he laughingly puts his knob back in-house, and tucking himself in again.
After Tony's floorshow, the attention moves to Ted. He doesn't really want to get his knob out, he knows he has a small one and the posh is going to make it look non-existent.

"Okay, you get your tits out and I'll get my knob out" Ted aims at Trudy, she thinks for a second or two.

"Okay in a minute." With that, she excuses herself and goes to the toilet. Ted doesn't really want to get his knob out in front of Bindi, he's always fancied her and doesn't want to put her off before he's even had the chance to shag her. (Not that that would ever happen, because Ted's happy in his relationship, he just likes the thought of it.)

So, while Trudy's away, Ted's catching up with Bindi as Tony scouts his collection of CDs for something else to listen to.

Ted finds out that she's settled in with her new job, got her own flat and is happy in a relationship that she's about nine months into now. "*Cool*" thinks Ted, who now doesn't feel under any pressure to impress, as she's now all loved up elsewhere.

Trudy returns down the pile carpeted stairs and parks herself back on the couch without looking at anyone. Ted and Bind still mull over the past and friends as the phone rings. Trudy picks it up, listens for a couple of seconds, and puts it down without saying a word.

This jogs Ted's memory. At his girlfriend's house where he's been spending most of his time over the last six or seven months, in the last few weeks there have been a number of occasions when the same thing has happened, the phone rings, Ted answers it, it goes dead.
"Must be a wrong number" she says. *"Sounds familiar"* Ted thinks.

He's now thinking of his girlfriend again. *"Shit."* He doesn't want to think of his girlfriend, he wants to think of fucking the arse off Bindi, and then he does...think of fucking the arse off of Bindi.
Trudy rudely interrupts Ted's fantasy.
"Right then, tits Ted! You want to see my tits?"

She stands up and turns around to face the wall. On the wall is a very large mirror. Lifting her top, out flop her tits.
She's now looking at her own reflection. Ted can't see them because she's got her back to him, so he has to see her by way of the reflection in the mirror, then he looks at her face. He notices that she's not looking at the reflection of herself at all, she's looking past herself to the curtains behind her. He looks directly at the curtains and notices that there's a very small gap between them, the curtains being not quite pulled shut. Ted realises she might be worrying that someone could look through the gap, see her standing there in full view, with her saggy tits out. Turning round and looking straight at Ted, she holds her top right up to her chin, and waits for the reaction.
"Whahay!" exclaims Ted. "Yeah, you got good tits!" Again Teds on his best behaviour.

"Well come on then, let's see your knob Ted!" she says, putting her saggy tits back into her heavily supportive showpiece bra. Ted wonders why she didn't go and pull the curtains properly.
Oh well, no point worrying about it, If she's fine with the curtains not being quite pulled, then so am I.
What sort of person's going to be standing out on the front lawn in the dark looking through someone else's front room window?

Ted gets up, undoes his belt, pulls his jeans down and shows off his British home stores briefs. Bindi starts laughing.

"What?" says Ted looking at her with his shorts still up.

"They look really comfortable" says Bindi in an honest tone.

"They are, why, do you want to try them on?" he says jokingly.

Bindi and Trudy laugh loudly without Bindi giving an answer.

"What underwear are you wearing then?" Ted asks.

"I'll show you if you like!" Bindi remarks giggling, while hauling her body forward, and out of the chair.

Bindi stands up and lifts her skirt, with the other hand she slowly takes off her knickers, handing them to Ted.

"Whehey! Cheers." He laughs loudly and looks at Tony as if say he's scored.

"Well you wanted to see them, there you go." she says with a naughty smile.

Ted looks at Trudy, who has a grin to rival another Cheshire cat.

He's a little surprised at what's just happened. He's thinking, *Bindi's got a boyfriend and yet she's just taken off her knickers and given them to me, which means she's not serious about tonight and it's all just a laugh, which is all good. Oh well, I've got to return the complement now, haven't I?*

Ted takes off his briefs and hands them to Bindi, who, laughing again, starts putting them on! *"Fuck! What the fuck's going on?"* Ted wonders excitedly.

Bindi, now with Ted's briefs on, stands up straight and loudly shouts,

"Yeah, they are comfortable, aren't they?"

By this time Trudy's laughing uncontrollably at Ted's knob, which of course resembles an acorn. He has a little giggle at himself, while trying to stretch his foreskin to get it back to an acceptable size.

"No fucking chance, mate" says Tony, shaking his head and laughing.

"Oh well, I'll put Bindi's knickers on to complete the task."

Ted's got one bollock hanging out one side, and one bollock hanging out the other, with his acorn trying to find a home in the front of the skimpy fabric.

He stands up straight and says,

"Well yours fucking well ain't!"

With this, all four of them are falling about laughing. Ted's feeling a proper prat at this stage, so he takes Bindi's knickers off, holding them out so she can swap back. Bindi says, while still laughing cheekily,

"I'd rather wear yours, they're loads more comfortable." The sight of Ted standing there with his acorn out is the funniest thing she's seen in years.

Ted makes a hand gesture to give them back, and Bindi reluctantly takes them off while showing just a little of her thigh handing them back.

Trudy pounces on the phone breaking Ted's uncomfortable stupor, quickly tacking it into the kitchen. After a few minutes, she returns with the phone and says it's for Bindi, however, she'd better take it upstairs as it's a personal call. Bindi looks puzzled, but does as she's told disappearing up the stairs with phone in hand.

The atmosphere in the lounge changed from fun time, to a strange, heavy atmosphere. After a short while and a few raised words, Bindi reappears at the top of the stairwell, looking angry and confused, slowly going down the stairs she grabs her coat, bag, and says she has to go.

Tony and Ted look at each other, looking puzzled, something's obviously kicked off, but what, and with whom?

Bindi stops by the front door looking angrily at Ted, just as she's about to open it. Ted looks back at her, not understanding why she's so angry... and what's more, staring straight back, deeply into Teds eyes. Shaking her head at him, she says "No," as if something's been said on the phone that she can't believe, but whatever it was, it's making her leave with bad thoughts regarding Ted, and the evening that didn't finish.

This makes Ted paranoid, something's made her go home, and what's more, it's him she seems to be pissed off with. Well, if he doesn't pick up on this one, then there's no hope for him. The front door closes, and a cars door slams, as it hurriedly drives off.

Ted looks at Trudy who for *some* reason's looking guilty.
"Weird?" Ted says, genuinely confused.
"I don't know what that was all about" he says looking at Tony.

"Neither do I" Tony says sitting there with his hands open and fingers outstretched.
"Well, I'm going to fuck off home too."

Ted takes his share of the posh, and gives Trudy who's now looking more than a little worried, a kiss on the cheek. Ted leaves, feeling like the whole night was bizarre to say the least. Turning the night's actions over in his head, he tries to overlook the fact that the whole evening was a mess, and pushes it to one side promising to himself never to be entertained at one of Trudy's 'Coke nights' again. Ted makes his way into the cold night, for the walk home.

Trying to make head or tail of what had just occurred, and at the same time needing to find normality in his coked up state, Ted decides he's not going to go home, instead, he's going to go and see Helen for the rest of the night, have a cup of tea, and a cuddle before sleeping off the abnormal evening. Arriving at the house, it doesn't look like she's in. Checking around the house for any sign of life or light, he realises that even though she said she would be in all night, she's not. Now then, Helen's a creature of habit, so going out when she says she'll be in is a bit odd. Her answer phone activates when he tries to contact. Ted leaves a message for her to contact him when she gets the message.

While at work the on the Monday, Ted mulls over the Friday's evening's proceedings in his mind. He knows something wasn't right, he just doesn't know what?.
"*What the fuck was that all about?...Still, no problem, nothing happened, no one shagged anyone, it was all a bit of harmless fun, and my conscience is clear.*"

Helen opens the door to Ted on the Monday evening after work, she doesn't even look at him, swanning away from the door, she leaves him standing there to make his own way in, and to shut the door behind.
"Hello babe" Ted says, pleased to see her as she disappears into the kitchen.
Helen just replies with a weak "Hi."
Sitting down on one of her lounge chairs and looking at the TV, Helen asks,
"Did you have a good time on Friday night, then?"
"Yeah, it was Okay" he replies.

She gets up and goes to the kitchen to make a cup of tea. Shouting, she asks,

"What did you do on Friday night then?"

"Oh, just went round to a mate's house and had a couple of beers."
"Oh yeah, which mates were they then?"

"I don't think you would know them, old school mates, anyway I came round and tried to phone you that night. Where were you?" he says trying to move the conversation along, to get out of the hole.

"I didn't feel very well and went round a friend's house"

"Who was that then?" Ted asks.
"Just an old friend, you wouldn't know them" she says in a sarcastic tone.

Helen comes back from the kitchen and looks Ted straight in the eye.

"Ted, I've been fucked about so many times by boyfriends in the past; you wouldn't do that to me, would you?" His heart starts to pound so hard he almost can't speak.
"What do you mean?" he says doing his damned hardest for her not to notice his panic.

"You know, cheat on me." she says in a testing way.
"No, why? What's brought all this on?"
"Nothing, I just wanted to make sure, that's all" she says knowingly, looking down at the floor.
"No babe, I haven't and wouldn't, I don't know what you're going on about?"

"Good!" she says, looking at the door to the kitchen.

Ted notices over the next few weeks the atmosphere considerably changes; it's uncomfortable. What's more, those dodgy phone calls when the caller hangs up become more frequent. This carries on for a good few days before one evening, whilst in the middle of watching Eastenders, Helen erupts like a volcano screaming at Ted that she's been hurt before, and doesn't want it again. Ted's sure they had this conversation a little while ago, so just thinks she's having a bad day.

"I saw you Ted! I saw you!" she shrieks.

This is one issue that's probably not a good idea to pursue, but Ted being Ted, he won't admit to himself that it's all about the other Friday night, so dismisses it, thinking his girlfriend's gone a little crazy. Ted can't sit there listening to her screaming at him just because she's had a bad day, so tells her to calm down, sort her life out, and he'll phone her tomorrow after work.

Giving it a couple of days, he's surprised in the fact that she hasn't phoned him yet, so tries phoning her. She answers the phone, and without even saying hello she tells him to "just leave it."

"Leave what?" he asks confused.

"Just leave it" she keeps saying, and puts the phone down.

Ted's confused to say the least. They haven't spoke for a couple of days, she was going off her head the last time they spoke, and to top things off, things really haven't felt right since that Friday night. Ted now knows there's something to address here, and the phone call doesn't seem to do the trick. He decides to go round to her place and find out what's going on.

Arriving at her house, he finds her to be out. *"Strange, her car's there."*

Now, as we know, Helen is a creature of habit, so why she's not in at this time of the evening during the week when she has work in the morning is a little strange, to say the least.

"She must be out with her mum doing a little retail therapy or something" he thinks settling down into the seat of his car. Ted remembers the last time they spoke, and thinks a peace offering would be a good start, so decides to get her some flowers and some of her favourite wine. Returning from the local corner shop armed with his offering, he sits and waits...he doesn't have to wait long.

An expensive black car pulls up to Helen's drive. *'Why would a foreign car be pulling into Helen's drive?'*

Ted watches closely as a well-dressed chap wearing a smart grey suit, with slicked back greasy hair gets out. Helen gets out the passenger side. Ted's only parked across the road, but she hasn't seen his car, with him in it, watching them. Ted now feels like a bit of an undercover private investigator. They walk round the front of the car and he slides his hand around her waist...pulling her closer to him. *"Fuck off! No fucking way!"* Ted's mind's going crazy with anger as it's obvious what's going on.

They disappear through Helen's front door while kissing hard. Ted watches as the door closes behind them. He's starting to feel sick. *"No fucking way!"* he thinks again.

Watching the windows for confirmation of his disbelief, he gets it. First the hallway light, then the lounge light, then the kitchen light. The kitchen light stays on for about five minutes, long enough to make a drink. It goes off, then the lounge light goes off, then the bedroom light goes on. *"No fucking way!"* he thinks again, as his anger heightens. The bedroom light goes off. Now the only light on is the hallway light. *"It's now only too fucking obvious what's going on here."* Ted's anger floods his mind causing the adrenalin to shake him almost violently.

Ten minutes pass and the bedroom light goes back on. This somehow makes him feel better; it means that this greasy bastard, who's in there with his *ex*, is not as good shag as he is, Ted goes for at least fifteen minutes.

The light in the lounge goes on. Ten minutes later the greasy bastard exits out the front door, gets into the car and slowly, contentedly drives off up the road.
Ted's fuming, he doesn't know what to do. After a few minutes of his mind raging, he manages to calm himself enough to drive home without setting fire to her house.

Before he's walked into his own front door he's reaching for his phone. Grabbing the receiver, he dials Helen's number. Not quite knowing what to say, and as controlled as he can be, he tells her what he's just witnessed. Of course she denies it, screaming in panic and tears, accusing him of being a stalker, then screams blue murder and threatens to call the police.
Poor old Ted, he didn't even know they'd split up. He knows now that he's been stitched up by Helen, and by Trudy good and proper. That evening round the Trudy's house was a fix, and it's become planer than the phone he's just about to slam down.

Ted's feeling low, abandoned, rejected, neglected, but what's worse... he's been shat on from a great height, by his so called friends. Ted needs a friend now, a friend he can trust. He goes round to see his mate Mark, to let off some steam and talk to someone who will listen. As he explains to Mark as to what he's witnessed, and what has happened, Mark looks at Ted while thinking deeply and says,

"Hang on a minute, I saw her in the car you've described well over two months ago, she was laughing and joking with some chap. I thought they were friends from work, and you knew him, that's why I never said anything."

"Fucking hell! It's been going on for a lot longer than anyone would know then" Ted says to his mate in amazement.

"It certainly looks like it, Ted" Mark says, looking a little sorry for his friend.

As it turns out, Helen had been doing the dirty on Ted for quite a while. She'd been having a relationship with this chap, (who's more financially secure by all accounts,) and between them they'd been planning this for quite a while. Helen had to split with Ted in a way that made Ted look bad, and in doing so making her look like the victim. It turns out that Helen was so concerned about what people thought of her, she couldn't cope with just ending the relationship for someone else, she had to make someone else take the shit. The plan had worked perfectly, so well infact, that Trudy thought she was the one who instigated the whole thing, but she hadn't, she was just an assistant in someone else`s plan...a master plan.

***

I did hear that Trudy had apologised for what she did to her long time old friend Ted, I heard that that Ted accepted her apology and is now working hard at his local psychiatrist to try and adjust to street life again, now knowing that he can`t trust his so called friends anymore... Anyway, back to Mack and his Chaing Mai episode.

Chapter 21

The day after yesterday

Day 9

Daylight streams through the gaps in the bamboo walls, circulating dust is visibly illuminated by the light. The room has no window, the ceiling fan hangs motionless in the same position as when he fell asleep. Mack lifts his arms stretching them out in front while sitting up, using his abs he pivots on his bottom swinging his legs to the side of the bed and planting his feet on the floor. Digging his phone from his pocket he checks... no messages.

Sliding the door bolt open, he pokes his head out. The air's heavy with heat coming from the outside like a radiator. Mack's toothbrush and other cleaning possessions are at the other guest house. Needing to freshen up, he spots two sinks at the far end of the corridor which he missed last night in the dim light. Mack now knows why the floor seemed spongy underfoot, it's an exterior wooden skeleton frame with a floor made of bamboo, with just a tarpaulin to cover it. The whole piece seems to be just plonked on the outside of the building to give access to the rooms. *Health and safety out here seems to be a little slack.*

Reaching the end of the corridor it changes to concrete, solid under foot. The old metal taps allow a slow run of cold water. Splashing it on his face he rubs the coolness round his neck. Feeling good, he repeats it. The T-shirt he'll be throwing away acts as a towel. As for his mouth, it resembles Ghandi's flip-flop. A quick rub round with water and his finger helps. The thought of an ice cool lemonade to moisten and bring his mouth back to life gives way to the thought of a fresher mouth.

Mack looks for a different exit from the entrance he came in last night, there's nothing worse than walking out first thing in the morning and getting nabbed, he has to be on his toes. However, checking all ways, there isn't one. He's got no choice but to exit via the main entrance. He's cautious, keeping his face down while again making full use of his peripheral vision. Wandering down the street, Mack starts to feel not too bothered now, in fact he's beginning to enjoy the feeling of being hunted and being alone again. Why?...because he's always been alone... brought up in a children's home, taught how survival works from a very early age.

The world's full of different people. Mack's just one of them. *'When the shit goes down, it makes no odds.'* Nothing detracts Mack from the hard core. He is the hard core, and if they think he ain't...they die, and more fool them.

Mack made the grade a long time ago. He wasn't born like it, he didn't even want to *be* the way he is, but he had to defend himself from the awards of court. The ones who were angry at being let down by their own parents, the ones who were angry at the system, those were the ones he had to defend himself against.

His early life set him up for life, life with the regulars and more with the specials, all these experiences basically forced him into the only job he knows how to do. He's a product of society now, a product of work, his destiny was written a long time ago by people who were never his blood, they were unknowingly setting him up to be the Mercenary that he now is.

If the shits going down they had to deal with it, not just with what's going on now, but with Mack's past too... As far as Mack's concerned... it's going down... and Mack doesn't care, he wants to put things right. They just don't know what wrong he wants to right... They think it's all about money and respect... How wrong could they be, and how little do they know about this man, and what they've now done to turn this situation into now their biggest nightmare.

It's now 'their' problem. These people have just tried to take him out, and in doing so they've made it personal.

Mack's got to stay focused though, he has to stay real, live by his word... or die because of stupidity. He hasn't got time for anything else now... only the job ahead.

Waiting for his instructions, he hopes he doesn't get any... he wants to go AWOL... just for the sake of it...like his now coherent and focusing mind... AWOL... adding death and destruction to the growing menu.

Finding a small empty restaurant a mile up the way just off Rat Chiang Saen road, he checks the perimeters, many escape routes present themselves.

A Koa Tom with poached egg for breakfast sounds good, and a coke. The lemonade doesn't seem to go with spicy soup, however, the egg does. Mack likes egg, it's rich in protein. *Some bread will soak this into a digestible lump, with plenty of salt.*
Mack likes his salt, brain food by all accounts... and it makes the food tastier. Knowing how his body and mind works, the brain food will give him the focus and drive he needs... with the knowledge of turning him back into the most efficient machine he can be.

This morning's thoughts were all very well, but it's not just himself he has to think about, and being reckless is unprofessional. He has a job to do, and it needs to be done properly and professionally...

Man United are one nil up playing Portsmouth on the TV. Mack's not into football, but it brings life back into perspective, it's in English, and it's from home.

Checking his phone... still no text or call, if he doesn't hear from the team by midday, then he'll make his own decision, as soon as the salt gives him the driven chemicals for the right decisions. The breakfast was tasty, even if the soup did make his eyes water. Sitting at the wooden table on the old wooden chair, Mack's chin rests in his palms with his hands round his cheeks, resting on the elbows. Loneliness is Mack's favourite state of mind, loneliness is the state of mind where Mack feels safe, he knows then, that the only person he has to rely on is himself. Loneliness also gives Mack the freedom of not having to worry about anyone... or anything.

Leaving the shelter of the restaurant behind, Mack looks to rent a motorcycle as travelling on public transport is too dodgy now.
A map catches the eye as he strolls past an empty convenience store. If he's going to make his own way back to Koh Phangan, he's going to need it. The maps size folds snugly into a compartment of his money belt, but now finding motorbike rental is priority.

Mack remembers seeing an advert somewhere for 'Joe's bike team.' They rent out 250cc trail bikes, which would be perfect for off road, just in case, and of course would suit any tarmac too. It comes to him... *Just off Chang Moi road.* Which is a little too near to the stadium for his liking, however needs must, he just has to be careful. The 'Joe's bike team' sign hangs over the window, a little worn and cracked by the heat, but it's the shop he needs and that's good enough, the only problem is...it's closed. A note blue-tacked to the inside of the glass in Thai and English writing tells Mack to phone a number, so he does.

"Hello, is that Joe?" He asks.

"No, it's Terry, sorry, Joe's not here, can I help?" comes the reply and sounding professional.

"Yeah, please mate, I want to rent a bike."

"Okay, we've only got an MZ250 at the moment."

"That'll be fine." Mack replies, thinking that it would be even less conspicuous, and can still handle the terrain well enough.

"Okay, how long do you need it for?" Terry asks.

"Just a couple of days." Mack says knowing that when he gets to Bangkok he's going to dump it anyway.

"Okay, I'll be down to the shop in five minutes. You'll need a full driving licence and your passport."

"Okay, I'll see you in a bit." Mack cuts him off checking his paperwork.

A roar from a trial bike five minutes later echoes down the quiet back street.

"Hello mate" Terry says once he's dismounted the bike and taken his helmet off. A well tanned man of about forty, the colour off his skin indicates that he's been in Thailand for quite a while. The wrinkled leathery face and gravelly voice speak volumes of his time spent in hot countries, and the amount of tobacco he smokes, with no doubt almost constant alcohol. Fumbling around with some keys on the key fob, the garage door opens inwards displaying an old looking, but very workable MZ250. It sits there in the sun, showing through the doorway... ready to transport him, red. *Well worn in, with all the necessary dials and metalwork which all look safe enough.*

"For this one, for a couple of days will cost you 800 baht, that's 400 a day." Terry says while mounting the seat and kicking the MZ into life, filling the small lock-up with blue exhaust fumes.

"Yeah, great!" Mack replies, coughing slightly on the fumes. "Can you do it on the card?" he shouts over the noise of the bikes engine.

"Yeah, no problem." Terry shouts back, turning the bike off.

Mack pays with the card supplied by the team. The passport details he hands over are also supplied by the team. Terry photocopies all the paperwork and sorts a snugly fitting helmet out. They have a quick chat about England, the difference in cultures, the weather, the Elephant riding and of course football, (which Mack has no interest in whatsoever) before Mack says his goodbyes and pulls off on the bike. The MZ's a heavy old thing, but Mack loves it, an old road bike that doesn't attract any attention and will go for ever.

Getting out of Chaing Mai's easy, straight down the 106, and with this bike, power or what? No one gets in Mack's way, he can only see which way he wants to go, a mental case, he's probably caused ten accidents... none of which he was involved in. The bike feels like it has a mind of its own and it's been waiting to get out for a ride for years, like a greyhound chasing the rabbit that it's never going to catch. If there's one thing an MZ is good at... it's to keep on going, never tiring, a trusted steed indeed... so long as it's got fuel.

He's thoroughly enjoying the journey. The fact that he's only been travelling for 20 minutes and has about 20 hours to go is beside the point. Mack's enjoying life again, he feels as free as a bird and now wants to stop somewhere to get a rare steak to eat, not because he's hungry, but because he feels like it. Just as soon as the thrill of this freedom of the road subsides, he'll stop for that steak.

Arriving at a small place by the name of Ban Hong, he finds a small open fronted restaurant... steak's on the menu, and if there's one thing he knows about the Thai's, it's that they'll always try to be accommodating, and they are.

The steak was delicious, rare, just how he wanted it. The fact that he probably just ate the muscles of an Alsatian dog, or horse is of no consequence, he's under no illusions, and it was good, filling him up to the point of contentment.

Full, happy, and under no stress... Bam! A black yellow striped plastic road bollard flies past the front of the restaurant. Mack doesn't move a muscle. The situation has to be sussed out, and fast. Flashing his eyes round the shack he looks for cover. Moving swiftly to the toilets he visited earlier gives him an exit if need be. His movements are fast and swift, the chairs and table don't give any noisy tell-tale signs of him leaving. His calf muscles felt the trigger. Mack hopes he hasn't pulled anything. His heart rate doubled with the explosion of energy, with the thud, the thud of blood pumping round his head with speed, It's loud, it's all he can hear. Controlling his breathing to bring his functions into a state where they're useful, not hampering, Mack slows himself down. Listening closely... no sound... no sirens... no shouting. Mack's eyes scan the front of both sides of the restaurant. The four wooden uprights holding the front of the restaurant up, stand there without life. He gazes towards the middle, slightly down the floor, back into the bar, the peripheral picking up any movement.

He waits and listens for a minute or so... nothing. Trying not to look conspicuous, Mack slowly makes his way to the front of the restaurant. Peering out...an old 4x4 with the owner looking concernedly at his front bumper, and then at the bollard. A couple of other people from other small shop fronts look at the incompetent driver, seeing what the commotion was. It's obvious that he's hit it accidentally, and to be honest...he's looking a little embarrassed. *Stupid wanker must have undercooked the brakes.*

Mack realises just how jumpy he is. What he needs to do now is get organised. Stopping for something to eat has given him a stark reminder of the fact that he's on the run. Mack decides it's time to stock up and take a break from village life. He looks for a shop that sells the provisions needed for a night out. A mini mag-light, one thing he didn't think he would need. The Swiss army knife he has is fine, he's had it for a whole week now, unlike the one he has at home, he's had that one for nearly twenty years, but was unable to get it on the plane. A blanket being the next thing, as it gets cold around four o'clock, a large towel will do the job. There are a few more things he needs before he leaves Ban Hong for Bangkok, one being... food.

Once Mack's stocked with all his essentials, he sets of again on the MZ. Having at least one stop overnight, he doesn't want to chance the hotels, motels or guest houses. From there, he has to make his way back down south. Here he anticipates the orders will be to track the fat man, get back the 50 euro printing plates, and smash this ring. Hopefully this will draw out the hit, and he can close this baby down once and for all.

Filling up the bike up cost a pittance, the float in the petrol pump brings back memories, he's only seen another one like that before, and that was a few years ago while he was working with a unit finding his way through Africa. With the tank full, it should get him all the way to Bangkok. Mentally checking himself before getting out of Ban Hong, he has...Beans x 2, water...two litres, Swiss army knife, a large towel, torch, a lighter for a fire and ciggies. Ciggies, insect repellent, (powder and spray) thick string, and of course...chocolate.

The sky turns a dull red and with the sun almost gone, Mack switches the lights on. He's been riding for five hours solid, the drone from the engine's become part of his hearing and his arse is starting to ache like a gigolo after a night on the job. He's ready for a break, as the air turns a little cooler and the mountains start to engulf the roadside around him further up, visible in the dim light by the roadside is a set of large boulders, with a nine or ten metre gap between them, right at the foot of those looming mountains. *A good place to camp* he thinks as he pulls the MZ onto the dirt. It rides easily over with the bouncing headlights giving plenty of light, directly on to where the front wheels aim. Oversized gaping shadows surround him, just showing in the dusk light that will soon, hopefully, give way to a clear and bright moonlit night. Behind the rocky boulders give a good all round view, but at the same time an obstructed one from the road, it provides good concealment. Pulling the bike to a slow stop, turning the key anticlockwise, all is quiet. The helmet slides off his head, and as it does, so the air swirls refreshingly around bringing his senses back, relieving his skull from its previously constricted housing.

In the quarter moon of night, his eyes adjust to the dull surroundings that slowly become visible.
Mack dismounts the machine, walking like a cowboy for a few strides as the blood returns to the legs and muscles, they start to work again. Sliding rucksack off his back onto his forearm, he then lets it fall to the floor.

The bike's become a reliable friend, giving off comforting heat, not that the nigh time temperature's not warm enough for him, but because he's bonded with the bike, he sets up camp next to it. With the help of the maglite he finds plenty of good hand sized rocks which he gathers in the towel, then he sets about organising his sleeping arrangements.

Hollowing out a small dip big enough for himself, he then digs a small trench around it spreading the entire contents of one of the powder insect repellents evenly within it, then sprays himself with the other. Now protected from unwanted guests in the night, he sits. Maglite in his mouth he takes out the beans, water and SAK. Piercing the can easily with the tin opener, he leaves the jagged lid by the bike. *Never know when you might need a jagged edge.* Stirring the contents of the can, mixing juices and solids into an edible consistency, he tips it to his dry lips, drinking water in between mouthfuls to minimise indigestion, and to make for a fuller, tastier meal, he saves the other can for the morning.

Mack looks around to see if he can get away with a small fire, and the search for things to burn is on... *If there's one thing that's in abundance around here... it ain't wood.* he thinks laughing to himself. Breaking a width of chocolate off and popping it in his mouth, he eats it slowly, enjoying the melting flavours that thicken the mouth, allowing it to thin out before swallowing. A cigarette in the loneliness of solitude is quite companionable; drawing hard on it causes the end to glow, which somehow eases his mind. The nicotine gets to work while letting his throat and lungs get in on the act, Mack enjoys the poison.

Mack's eaten, drunk, had a sweet and a cigarette, he enjoys his four course meals, always has. Getting up and stepping outside the sleeping arrangements, small and medium rocks are needed to surround the dip. After finding what he was looking for, the dip`s now surrounded by a small solid barrier, pushing the dusty soil into the gaps of the rocks, the banger is complete, a cosy little wind breaker. The rucksack acts as a pillow and the towel a blanket. Checking the phone...no messages, no calls, and no signal.

The new phone has games programmed in, so a new high score on space invaders is called for. Another piece of chocolate, a cigarette, a few slugs of water and the evening's ready for Mack to enjoy, as he beds down staring up into an infinite night sky... no clouds, no light pollution, just trillions of stars, the world as he knows it... and loves.

Chapter 22

A Rude Awakening

Day 10

A great night's kip he thinks opening his eyes to the morning. The light is just bright enough to see as he turns to put his elbow into the ground. A hiss comes from behind. Mack knows exactly what the sound is, and what it means.

Slowly, very slowly Mack turns his head. Two to three feet away... *A viper, not a cobra, it doesn't have the wide neck, it's a chain viper and deadly none the less. If I get a bite from this baby it could all be over.* Manoeuvring himself into a crouching position while keeping fluid movements, he stays low as his eyes stay glued to the reptile. The viper hisses loudly as if to say he's the top dog at that present time, Mack sees things differently.

He doesn't *have* to kill the snake, he doesn't *need* it for food, but at the same time Mack *doesn't* like to be threatened before he's had his breakfast. Looking at the markings, *Chain viper or not, you die.* Keeping low with bent knees, he slowly crosses one foot out of his banger diagonally across his body and over the other to move sideways, keeping his arms outstretched for balance. Repeating the movement trying to get round the reptile he's now on its left side. It follows Mack, but only with the top eighth of its body, Mack's almost there, he can see the tail.

Moving his top body weight towards the snake...it darts forward a few hissing inches, not worrying Mack too much. Mack needs to draw its body out longer knowing how les mobile a snake is once drawn out, so sways back and forth in momentum to unsettle the reptile further, and also for Mack to be in constantly motion for a quick drawback if necessary. He calculates that the tail can be reached, again he inches forward in momentum...the snake hisses lunges and recoils, demanding Mack's reflexes to do the same. Undeterred by the hissing reptile he again moves slowly towards the tail, and with lightning speed Mack makes a grab for it...just as the snake also makes an attacking lunge...they both miss...a stand-off. He can feel the snake's persona, it doesn't want to be there any more, it now knows that it's found an aggressor...not a victim. *But hey, too late now son!*

Mack's enjoying the rush as they look deeply into each other's eyes, both knowing now that this is to an untimely ending. Mack gets a little closer, the reptile may be drawing Mack in for the kill. Strike! the reptile lunges forward as Mack pulls his arm in like he's just pulled it from a fire. *Fucker! He nearly had me then.*

He feels like a Sioux Indian doing a bizarre reptile dance as his swaying and bouncing continues. Mack strikes grabbing the tail, and in one swift motion the snake lifts off the dirt and is being swung round Mack's head. He's now running towards the rock mound swinging the reptile round and round his head like a cowboy with a lassoo... screaming a loud 'yeeha!'... Wham! He smashes the reptile onto the rocks. Not letting go he runs round again like a victory lap and wham! - repeats the process. Running around for his third lap of victory, he lets it go. The snake flies spinning in the morning air towards the mountains, coming to rest with a thwoping sound, kicking up the dust... it lies motionless. Looking at the dead carcass he wanders up to it emotionless, standing over it for a few seconds to take in the death fight memories that ensued only a few seconds earlier. Then he starts dancing round the dead reptile doing a 'dead reptile' celebration ritual that involves throwing his arms in the air and hoping from one foot to the other. Mack's mind set has changed; he has a laugh to himself. *If the lads could have seen that, hahahahaa!*

Sitting back in the Banger he retrieves the map from his money belt, then locates the tin of beans and repeats his meal from last night. He packs the rucksack, sparks up a ciggie mounting the bike and pushing it off its stand. With the rucksack on his back, he finishes the cigarette while admiring the Thai morning tranquillity that resembles the Grand Canyon, but without the Canyon. (not that he's ever been there). Flicking the butt into the now disused Banger and blowing the remnants of smoke from his lungs...so that his helmet doesn't stink of smoke, he puts the helmet on, and kicks the bike into action.

Back on the tarmac again he rides through Nakhon Sawan stopping for a while to have an egg and chips dinner, he then travels down the '1' Phahon Yothin. On this stretch things start to become a whole lot busier, it gets to the stage where it reminds him of his journey out of Bangkok a week or so earlier, only this time it's still light, and he's the rider. A little while later he's parking the bike just down the road from Khao San Road, leaving the bike with the keys in the ignition and the helmet on the handle bars...he walks away. *A present for someone.*

Khao San is a place for the 'Farang', meaning tourist. Bright lights and flashy prostitutes litter the street, open bars with the largest gathering of westerners in Bangkok. Here you can get food, restaurant or food off the stalls, sex, booze, hotels, motels, guest houses. You can get beaten up here, killed, maimed, you can get drugs, clothes, ornaments, presents...and you can also get ripped off.

It's busy, with the air thick of testosterone. Mack finds an open fronted restaurant. Ordering a coke, he watches as a fight breaks out amongst a group of Thai ladies in the middle of the street. He doesn't know what it's about, but it's entertaining anyway. Drinking the coke, he checks his phone. A message came through over two hours ago.

:Return call: Mack knows this is from the team. He thumbs in the number.

"Hello" the voice answers.
"Sticky." Mack replies with the code word he uses.
"Will call back in five" the voice replies, and the line goes dead. Five minutes later his phone vibrates.
"Sticky" Mack says as he answers.
"Where are you?"
"Bangkok" Mack replies.
"Okay, Good. Intelligence tells us the plates are going to be with the fat man. You were stitched up, they wanted you captured and interrogated, then probably disposed of somewhere. They don't know who you are, or who you work for. The fat man suspected you when you were in Koh Phangan the last time, it seems you took care of a couple of his men a little too well for a standard courier. He used his influence with Special Branch to try to get you captured. Go to Koh Phangan and recover the plates, this should draw Christophe out, capture him if you can, and we'll arrange for extraction."
"Understood." Mack replies, and cuts the team off.

Nice. Mack thinks. *Payback time!*

Chapter 23

Plans

The fight with the Thai ladies fizzles out. The police turn up, just loud voices are now being exchanged with a few pointed fingers. Mack looks at the menu. Bacon and eggs, egg and chips, chips and... *Blimey they're certainly set up for the westerners around here, or what?* Mack orders ham egg and chips. He doesn't feel like he has to eat Thai food just because he's in Thailand... let's face it, he's not on holiday... any more.

Browsing the map to plot the route down to Surat Thani, his English fry up gets plonked on the table beside him, with the plate covering the corner of the southern island. Mack digs in with his knife and fork splitting the yoke which seeps into the boiled rice. An egg on boiled rice just doesn't quite hit the mark. Deciding that the food's crap, he wanders down Kao San Road looking for a hotel.

Koa San is buzzing for the time of day, stalls selling everything line the pedestrianised road. People are shopping for tack, others are having their hair braided, platted, washed, coloured, basically anything to make them stand out and look like they've been to Thailand. Gap year university students sit in circles drinking Chang, Singha, trying the musical instruments, trying to fit in and speak with their "way out man" lingo, chilled attitudes and long rollicking laughs, like they've been smoking the local herb for the past six months, and have lost sight of the western world. Bongo drums play close by, creating an almost carnival atmosphere. At least it's a relaxed and happy one, considering what goes on here...It's a good vibe.

Mack doesn't fancy breakfast with a snake in the morning, he fancies tasting a bit of luxury for a change, there's no rush. *It'll be at least another day or so before the plates get to the fat man, so it's recuperation time for me.*

The Viengtai Hotel lights up at the end of the road, it stands like a palace compared to what he's been used to of late, tonight this looks like Mack's kind of place. *Only a four star, but it will be fine I'm sure.* 2100 Baht later he's in his room. *More like a twenty star!* he thinks as he gazes around at the well furnished and more than accommodating room.

The hotel room has full sat TV... in the lounge... which adjoins the bedroom, which has a fantastically fitted out en suite. He spreads the map out on the bed, *Now then, car hire?* Plotting his route down to Surat Thani, the thought of meeting the fat man again makes his blood race as this time it won't be so pleasant. Running a bubbled up bath, he pours the liquid from the scented bottles in too, he lays back, allowing himself to enjoy the warmth, tucking a well-trodden toe up the cold-water taps spout.

Fully soaked, relaxed and smelling good, he's back on the streets of Bangkok to purchase new attire. The street stalls offer all the stuff he needs. He buys new three-quarter length slacks with plenty of pockets, a short-sleeved shirt, trainers...and this time, sunglasses...Ray-ban, they don't come any moodier.

Day 11

A fresh morning air blows the hairs on his arm flat as it rests on the edge of the Tuk-Tuk's armrest. Mack enjoys the morning air, bright clear and clean, a freshness that by midday turns to something quite different. A morning like this makes it all feel new again, and fully charged. The Euro car sign hangs out from the forecourt. Its green and cream oval shape reminds Mack of the next piece of equipment he's going to need for the next leg of his journey. The car's waiting for him, parked out front, freshly washed and glinting brightly in the sun. The silver stream lined aerodynamics and alloy wheels make him anticipate comfort on his journey down to Surat Thani. It's a Honda Civic and he's got it for seven days. The air con works well, turning the outdoor heat of a fire, to the inside temperature of a fridge, and no doubt when he gets it onto the open motorway, it'll tick along nicely.

Mack makes his way out of the city and onto the '35'. A few hours later he's changed onto the '4'. The egg on toast he enjoyed while stopping at Ton Maphrao satisfied his hunger very well indeed, he still misses the good old Tommy K to go with it though. A stroll he took round the village to walk off the breakfast proved fruitful. Sitting on the passenger seat are his essentials. Water, cigarettes, wine gums, and a David Gray CD, 'White Ladder', an album he's always wanted to listen to... thoroughly. *There's nothing better than to chill out, with some soothing tunes, air-con, with the beautiful sights of Thailand going by, while chewing on a wine gum. Yep...living the dream.*

The journey brings him to Chang Raek. A break for tea, then on to Surat Thani, which he reaches after dark. Mack doesn't want to stop for directions, he's enjoying the tune 'Babylon' too much and to interrupt it would be a sin. Not only that, he likes the way the cars dials illuminate in the dark.

After an hour of trying to find his bearings and listening to 'Babylon' twenty or so times, the pre-booked Khao Sok hotel's lights shine like a beacon for a now welcome break. He didn't know it was on the side of a mountain. After checking in and being shown to his accommodation, disappointment sets in a little, after being spoilt the night before in the Bangkok Ritz, It just seems a little crap, Mack will get by though, however, there's no air-con, only ceiling fans. *A little tight, considering its well over £10 a night.* It doesn't matter though, Mack has to get settled, he needs to get over to Ko Samui tomorrow. From there he'll charter a boat and get to Koh Phangan, and then on to recover the 50 Euro plates. There's no doubt in his mind that he'll be bumping into the Turks again... and maybe a few others along the way. Flicking the switch by the bed, Mack puts his head down for the night.

Morning wakes him, while staring at the ceiling with his head resting on his hands, he's had time to put together a plan of action, and to work out the provisions he's going to need. So, shopping is first on the list after the full breakfast, and a cup of tea.

At least four devices will be needed to slow people down, or create a diversion once at the villa. This is the sort of stuff you don't just walk in and buy off the shelf in a superstore, he's going to have to make his own plastic explosives, and after a good few hours trawling the shops, he comes back with what he needs...
Petrol
Plastic bags
Oil
A large glass bowl
G*******R
G*******N
Four small battery alarm clocks, and of course some rather nice nuts and bolts. The gunpowder he'll also make out of Potassium nitrate, charcoal and sulphur, and a few other bits and bobs to make the detonators, all of these he's managed to purchased from various shops in Surat Thani. As for fire arms, *let's hope I bump into the Turks again.* Mack sits down at the table. He makes sure the shutters are closed, and then sets about constructing the lethal devices.

By late afternoon the pack's ready, four plastic explosive devices, all ready to set for detonation. The next meeting will be with the unforgiven underworld that tried to bump him off while in Chaing Mai. Mack is willing and able, he's looking forward to the next rendezvous. Remembering the last time he was at the port in Surat Thani, he knows that when returning the car will need to be close by. Parking it near the large coach stop, he jumps on the last boat out to Koh Samui.

Arriving at Koh Samui, the taxi to take him to the Chaweng residence for the evening waits. The room again is relatively basic, however, it's on the second floor, and the hotel has a small swimming pool which his veranda overlooks. Showered, and fully satisfied with the local cuisine, Mack sits by the pool with a new map of Koh Pangan, studying it thoroughly the thought comes to him as he plots his plan, route, and a rough idea of how it's going to happen... tomorrow the fat man *will* sing.

Returning to his room and the fan turning to create a light breeze, he nods off.

Day 12

Mack wakes to a sharp pain on the side of his head...he's just banged it...on the underside of a ceramic sink. Finding himself crouched under it, disoriented and confused, the memories of the Adoo soldiers and the sound of the strike master jets letting go their rounds slowly fade. He's sweating badly and becoming conscious of where he is. *Fuck!* he thinks as he crawls out from under and out of his bunker. Running the cold tap, the cold water on his face and neck now wake him fuller. The visions of the bloodied mangled bodies of his two friends he lost while scrapping were there again, It still haunts him, and always will. He spits between his teeth while looking at the wall... *Fuckers!*

Feeling the cool liquid drain from his hands, he stands there, elbows resting on the sides of the sink, his face rests in his hands. Mack hates this part of the aftermath, he was never given the diagnosis of posttraumatic syndrome that the modern day soldier have the benefit of these days.

No...Mack has to deal with it his way. He doesn't know what way that is, because it just doesn't seem to get any easier. In fact, the more time that goes by, the more time he has to sleep, the more he just slips back to the realms of death, destruction, and the feeling helplessness, being pinned down by enemy fire as one of the units he worked with slowly disintegrated around him, because of shit intelligence.

Looking at his toothbrush and toothpaste, all he knows how to do is to do the next thing he has to do. This time, it's to clean his teeth, get his shit together, and move on.

The pool has a surface tension on it that you could walk on, like a pane of glass, he strides past it on his way for breakfast down at reception. The paper rack holds the Daily Mail...from a week ago. Reading the front page and glancing into the reception, looking for a place to sit at the tables and chairs, he can't believe his eyes, who's sitting at one of the breakfast tables?... *Ennis the fucking Turk.* Not having been spotted, Mack has time to move from view, around the corner. *No problem for now,* he thinks. *They don't know I'm here,*

they don't know what's on the agenda, and they suspect nothing...
I'll just have to bide my time.

The element of surprise is Mack's greatest allied. To ruin it would mean that it would all be over. Mack now knows he has to be very, very careful indeed. Getting around the islands without being seen or suspected is crucial. He now knows that the Turks are floating around, which isn't a bad thing, because if they're here in Samui, then they're not with the fat man. He has to jump the island without being seen. Darkness is now the safer option, which now means he's got plenty of time to check his pack, himself, and make sure he's in peak performance.

Waking at five in the evening and trying the reception area again, he finds that it's clear. Cautiously Mack makes his way to the port, and on arrival he's greeted by the huge bay and sandy bars that line the circumference. They're great cover as he meanders his way through picking up on the holiday vibe while keeping an eye out for the Turks, and a boat rental.

Five or six boats moored a little further out look like they could cut a channel in the Indian ocean without breaking a sweat. They'd get him there and back in no time. Scanning the front bar for any sign of boat rental, a sign advertising trips to the island of Koh Pangang and the full moon party grabs his attention. Mack walks up to the Thai chap who sits under the sign.

"Hello mate, can you take me to Koh Pangang?" he asks, while scouring for Turks. An English chap sitting on a little further up cuts in...

"Hello mate, where are you going?"

"Just over to Koh Phangan. I'm meeting some friends at Had Rin beach for a party." Mack replies sounding touristy.

"Well it's a bit late to be going now innit? There's no full moon party tonight anyway?" comes the reply.

"I know, but I promised I would be there for the evening, I can only stay the one night." Mack says with a 'c'mon mate do me a favour' attitude. The chap thinks for a little.

"Okay, but I can only take you one way, you'll have to come back tomorrow. I'll give you a number to phone for that if you want?"

1500 baht he says, knowing that Mack has no choice.

"Yeah, Okay" Mack replies, knowing he's being ripped off.

He was right, that boat cut a channel through the Indian ocean like it wasn't even there. Mack changes his mind from going to Had Rin, to Thong Sala, it would be a safer stop, as it's a lot busier and he can lose himself in the bustle of things, rather than wade into shore from an isolated boat, coming into the fat man's beach. Not only that, having been to the port before, Mack knows just where to go for bike rental. The rental shops are still just about open as the light fades and the dim bar bulbs show signs of the nightlife waking. The rental shack's shutters are just about to come down, but he manages to get a 125cc moped before the corrugated shutters block his needs.

The bike's almost the same as the last one he rented. It's a little older, a different colour, and not as tight, but it does the job just the same. The machine putts its way towards Had Rin confronting the steep gradient that had him worried when he was travelling in the 4x4 the last time he came, it demands leaning over the headset for a counter balance. Drawing nearer to the fatmans territory, Mack decides to park the bike up a good distance, and make the rest of the journey on foot. Retracing the journey he travelled with the Turks only a few days earlier, he keeps close to the trees as he approaches, stopping just far enough away so as not to look like he's scouting the area, he can now see the lights glowing from the villa. Mack starts towards it knowing this is the beginning of the real deal, a deal to end the fat man's reign.

Chapter 24

Boom

With the sun completely disappeared, if it were not for the moon illuminating his passage, seeing where he was going would be impossible. Mack had only quickly surveyed the surroundings at his last visit so this time he has to make a more detailed recce. Shadows could easily mislead the true nature of the landscape, or infact the obstacles he'll encounter tomorrow. The climate's close, making him feel very much at home, especially now that *their* hit, has become the hitman.

Feeling his way around the perimeter of the fat man's grounds, an old outhouse around the back comes into view that's almost totally obscured by trees, it can only just be made out by the trained eye. It's a solid structure with straight edges and sharp corners standing out from the trees and scrub land. Looming trees seem to have grown around it, their huge heavy leaves resting on its roof. Mack quietly makes his way towards it. A wooden door with an extremely heavy padlock connected to solid steel hinge bars keeps any unwanted intruders.

Well...the padlock's pretty well made, and doesn't look like it would make for easy pickings either. The door itself would be easier to go through than trying to pick the lock, noisy though.

Mack's intrigued. *Why would there be an outhouse that's so well secured, unless of course there's something in there of some importance?* Checking around the side of the outhouse he finds that on the adjacent side there's another door with no handle. He knows that it's able to be opened because of the three steel hinges that are attached to it. A well-paved path leads off down the mountain meandering out of sight. Mack wants to know where it leads, and of course get to the bottom of what the shed business is all about. Following the path along its dusty side he slowly starts the steep gradient down the hill back to the sea. The stone path changes to steps as the gradient becomes too steep, now, Mack can see right to the bottom, to where the steps stop right at the base of the climb. The ocean laps up against the solid uprights of what hold the jetty up and onto the rocks that surround the area.

But it's not the path and wooden jetty that Mack's looking at now, its what's attached to the jetty...a boat, and not just any old boat either... it's a Bayline power cruiser. Mack's always dreamt of owning a Bayline power cruiser, and what's more, it's a 3055, recognising it in the moon light is a synch. An arrow in the water when in full throttle, it's at least £100,000 worth and that's second hand. Mack also knows the ignition system on these babies. Whatever happens he wants a go in that boat. The getaway's now sorted, by all accounts.

Climbing the steps back up to the villa the lights from its brightly lit veranda shine like a lighthouse showing the way, also lighting the way *into* the villa, which is even more obvious now, straight through the front doors. Mack knows the front room is huge and the doors always seem to be open, he knows the layout, he's been there before.

Mack moves with stealth round the front of the villa while keeping an eye on the front room and getting close. The fat man sits on one of the couches spreading his fat body as he takes up the room of two people. He's alone, eyes closed, and obviously enjoying the classical music which pours from the very expensive media system expertly installed. Mack has a good look, scanning the lounge, dinning and kitchen areas. The Turks don't seem to be there. Not only that, the 4x4 isn't parked outside.
This is the perfect opportunity to take the shit-head out. However, Mack needs to locate exactly where the plates are. What's more, he may not be alone so again, caution is the name of the game.

Deciding he needs a closer vantage point, he closes in on the front balcony, straddling the glass wind-breaker and reaching the large open window without a sound. Managing to get close enough without the fat man even opening his eyes adds to his confidence, as from where he is right now, he could spit on him.
Mack's ready to get behind the fat man, grab him and choke the fat bastard to death, but that wouldn't do any good, as he needs the plates. But as a prayer gets answered, the man opens his eyes, and getting up walks out of the room.
Perfect! Mack thinks as he starts his silent sprint through the doors, across the stone floors to almost become the fat man's shadow, stopping at the doorway entrance to the hallway as Mack watches the man disappear through a doorway, closing it almost fully behind

him. Mack moves to the door, and carefully casting an eye through the gap sees the big man standing over a red/ blue tasselled rug. Half the rug is pulled back showing a large silver safe top, which is wide open. With his cumbersome sweaty hands, the blob removes things from the hole in the floor, placing them on the area around the safe lid, still rummaging around inside looking for something else.

The sound of a vehicle pulling to a halt out the front induces an almost panic state in Mack. *Shit!... Sounds like a 4x4, and the Turks.* If he tries to exit the building he'll be seen and all hell will break loose. Unlike them, Mack has no gun, cover needs to be found, and quickly.

Taking long strides on the balls of his feet, three large leaps take him to the far end of the corridor where he can be lost in the shadows. The Turks brashly make their way into the villa whilst talking loudly and laughing excitedly. Mack realises his cover won't be enough. Looking around quickly, he spots a wooden linen box which looks just large enough for him to fit in, just so long as he curls up...tight. Leaping to it he opens the lid to find it nearly empty, *good, enough room for me.* He hops in hoping the cleaner doesn't turn up to change the beds within the next short while.

The Turks voices get louder as they get closer, but there's another voice accompanying them, and what's more, it has a French accent. *A voice with an accent, a French accent, it can't be?... there's only one man involved with this lot with a French accent, and he's the one we're after, it's the fucking hit man! I can't fucking believe this, it's Christophe!* he thinks not believing his luck and listening intently.

The conversation's about Mack, and the switch that went sour in Chaing Mai. *He's obviously just been picked up from Koh Samui airport, that's why Ennis was there this morning.* This settles Mack even more now, because that definitely means that they don't know of his presence on the islands, and they weren't looking for him, it was just a coincidence that they were there.

The Turks talk about the last time that Mack was on the island, telling the Frenchman how dangerous Mack can be, explaining the road fight. Mack takes this as a complement, and thinks it's nice of Ennis and Ally to say so.

They sat in that lounge and chatted for what seemed like hours to Mack, but inevitably, they would make their way to the fat man's favourite restaurant so that he could show off the respect the locals pay him, and of course to flash some cash. The music stops and voices fade as they leave the villa. The sound of the huge French doors being slid home, then a click as they're locked gives the all clear. However, Mack now realises that he's now... locked *in*.

Okay...maybe the doors don't always stay open. he thinks opening the lid to what has been his home for the last hour or so.

Wincing in pain as the blood starts its journey back through the veins in his legs, he leans against the wall. Standing upright and finding his balance, he waits long enough for his legs to tingle back to life so his body can be ready for action. Not that it needs to be, however, a good look around to reacquaint himself with the battleground, and find where the plates are, or might be, is priority.

A door on the end wall of the corridor can just be made out in the dark shadows. Mack tries the handle to find it unlocked. Slowly he opens it to a black void. Mack feels the inside of the wall looking for a light switch. Running his palm down the wall he connects with a solid switch sunk into the wall, he flicks it down. Another corridor brightly illuminated by sunken ceiling down lights become apparent, a black flagstone floor with nothing but white walls either side, and steps at the end leading to nowhere. Mack wonders why there would be a corridor with no doors, or infact why steps at the end, seem to lead to nowhere. Attentively he follows it to the end and, looking up, sees a wooden hatch. Mack ponders, trying to fathom its existence there, and the fact the it sports a rather large bolt. Sliding the bolt out of its housing, he pushes the hatch up an inch to have a look.

Peering through the crack, Mack realises this is the wooden outhouse that leads down the steps to the Bayliner. Opening the hatch fully and without making a noise, he lowers it gently down, climbing out and onto a wooden floor. Two doors come into view, one without bolts and the other door with two. The two bolts slide out effortlessly and quietly, opening the door he peers out to the island's insects noisy playtime.

Yep, as I thought, an escape route... nice.

Locking everything back up and retracing his steps back to the now quiet and empty lounge, Mack knows that someone's looking down on him tonight, he's been very lucky so far and knows that without the help of that all-powerful existence that has looked after him all his life, he would probably not still be alive. However, his job goes on and next he needs to find where the plates are? They would probably be in the safe. Going to the bedroom where the fatman was earlier and pulling back the rug, a well-situated and solid safe that's concreted into the ground greets him. A square flat silver metal lid shields its contents. Lifting it, eleven touch pads and a key hole are showing off their complexity, showing its almost impenetrable existence.

There's no way I can get into this. The fat man will have to open it, he's probably the only one who knows the code, and has the key.

Deciding that tonight would be a good time to rig the villa, Mack slides the rucksack off his back (that took up too much room in the linen box for his liking) and resting it on the floor, unclips the top locating the lethal devices inside. The underside of the large dining table is his first stop. He duck tapes a device to the centre of it. (People rarely check the underside of a table, or clean it) The clocks have no battery in; however, they're all set for ten minutes after activation once the batteries have been installed, which he'll do at the time of the hit. He tapes another of the small solid devices to the underside of the linen box, and another to the underside of the bed in the fat man's room, the last being rigged in the wooden outhouse. With the villa fully loaded, the explosions will be enough for the gas mains to go...and then *bon voyage* to the roof.

With all devices in place and a plan set in his mind, he makes his way to leave before reading the room its last rights. (A habit he picked up along the way) Trying the French doors, he finds they're locked. This no good, because if he unlocks them from the inside, then he won't be able to lock them from the outside, which will alert the fat man to someone's presence. He has to find another way out... easy enough, the windows adequately accommodate Mack's exit, without a trace.

Chapter 25

The Nutter Returns

Looking back through the door of the open beach hut that is no more than half a mile from the villa, he checks that there's nothing to give away the fact he stayed there last night.

Resting his arse on an old wooden stool in front of the hut, he uses the binoculars bought in Surat Thani to check the Bayliner's still moored...it is, and glints in the sun like a sparkling diamond ready to be purchased...or nicked.

Mack does a last full check before setting off. The rucksack containing all he needs sits well on his back. The batteries for the devices are zipped up in his square thigh pocket.

Mack feels relaxed today, the sun's as hot and bright as always, and the food he ate last night is still working for him. He's wearing his trainers, snugly fitting with the laces in a double bow, ankle socks feeling comfy and tight. The three quarter length green camouflage trousers are a perfect fit, coming just below the knee, with the toggles around the bottom at a perfect tension. The strong black leather belt keeps the trousers at a good height, which are just above the waist for plenty of movement. The racing green T-shirt hangs at an angle, not restricting him. The cap soaks up any sweat and the peak shields the glare of the sun from his eyes.

Mack's ready to rock and roll. A good drink of water to hydrate himself and he'll be ready for the day's proceedings. Checking his Omega seamaster automatic chronograph watch that goes below 300 meters in the water, and boasts a power reserve of 44 hours... he's now on course for good timekeeping. He needs to be surveying the villa for midday, that's when he can lay low, get positioned, and plan the strike.

Taking a leisurely walk around the sandy bay, tourists are relaxing, playing football. The girls drink alcohol as they rub themselves up with coconut sun cream oily factor two, they play Frisbee showing off their superb figures while the sun warms and tans their superbly smooth skin. Their coloured beach towels give them a carpet to lie on, separating them from the sticky sand that always gets into crevices, that become an unwanted irritation.

They have no worries, just pure indulgence in relaxation and fun.

Looking up at the villa, which is easily visible, the reflection gleams like a peak of perfection ready to be dissolved by the day's future actions. It looks calm and majestic, unobtrusively looking out to the fantastic Indian Ocean. Mack sits down. The sand's warm, soft, the sea's sparkling with reflective sunshine. Movement, calm...the splash on the beach every four waves acts as sound therapy.

The water bottle's not as cold as it was. His strong hand squeezes a couple of gulps into his mouth as he looks up at the villa again. Resting his arms on his tanned hairy knees he knows that all this calmness will be rudely disrupted by the carnage that his future actions will create. Mack feels almost sad, knowing that this will be the case.

There's a lot of money riding on this deal though, and if the plates end up in the right hands, then the bonus they'll receive will make life a whole lot easier for all concerned. This situation is not to be taken lightly in any way shape or form, this could mean death.

Mack knows how much he loves his daughter, he also knows that this is what he does... to give his daughter the chance in life he never had. To be able to afford her college, university, a car that she can be proud of, the lessons to drive that car, and also a place to live...not near the shit-heads he had to put up with. A chance for her to be someone he could never be. The daughter he wants her to be, but would never force upon her. Mack's job is to provide options for her. This is why Mack fights, it's all he knows how to do. Fighting was his early lessons in life, these lessons for his beautiful innocent daughter is a no-no, he's making the change.

He knew when he was a child what was right and wrong, and he's more than prepared to fight to the death for this change for her, it's the least his daughter deserves. If her Dad won't do it, then who the fuck else will?

Mack wonders if his daughter would ever understand. He knows she wouldn't, she wouldn't understand because she would never have the facts, so how could she understand? She would never know his situation or his life. Mack has to make this pay, or the whole thing's a waste of time. He's got himself this far, and now it's time to take it further. He wants to write a letter, but he can't even do that. If he did, he would not return. This is it, shit or bust, and Mack knows it.

Anticipation hangs heavily in the air, building with every second. When it reaches the full level of expression... the deal begins.

***

My need to go to the toilet gets stronger with every second. This however eases slightly with the scent of the two girls in front, as much as they look good, it's the smell they give off, enough for any man's loins to stir.

Chapter 26

The Twins

They both wear identical black leather sensible shoes, which I imagine house small and perfectly formed toes connected to delicate feet, which are dressed in black tights (maybe stockings). They have nicely shaped calf muscles, that's all that can be seen because of their black skirts that come just below the knee, made of cotton I think... tight, figure hugging forms making the smooth feminine stomach visible.

My mind wants to get to know the personal details of these two. Why not, it's my mind and I can think what I want ... Imagine what I want.

If one was to remove the skirt... smooth skin with tiny soft hairs, the ones that one can only feel with the tip of the top lip and the end of one's nose. Slowly, hardly touching, dragging over the skin, moving the face up and breathing out through the nose as one passes the navel area. The stomach spasms very slightly with the touch of a moist tongue wanting to know the heat temperature of the skin.

Fingers finding the wide belt made of leather with a big square silver buckle, not easy to undo but not too difficult either. She just has to breathe in at the right moment as the index finger slips under the concave of the loose leather in front of the buckle. Gently pull the leather; it slips effortlessly out of its buckle. Hold the belt firmly and pull; out comes the pin from its leather housing. Tuck the index finger behind the pin and let the belt undo and. fall to the ground, circling the sensible shoes. The belt now is now redundant, lifeless, discarded.

Slowly pulling the white blouse up from inside the skirt and lifting it, out comes the smooth fabric on fabric sound, it drops over the skirt, it now also effortlessly.

An open flat hand firmly works its way up the front of the twins' skirt, just above the pubic area onto the waistband of the skirt, and touches the bare flesh; warm, smooth skin welcomes the rough palms. Extending the hand up towards her tits, the bone of her bra is firm; the warmth of her breast is just detectable through the rough feeling material.

Cupping the firm rounded warmth, the consistency is firm, big and rounded, convex, the perfect shape of one's imagination. This collection of sensitive pleasure mounds *have* to be released from their restricting bone meshed material prisons. They ache to be touched, needed and stroked, to engulf the owner in the realms of pleasure.

Holding the bottom of the blouse with both hands, one slowly pulls it up the body, rolling it over the red material nudging the warm soft topside of the material that holds the focal point to its perfect shape. The glories of the twins' undergarments are on show, proving to the hungry eye... their true beauty.

The buttoned blouse rises to her face. Small feminine fingers undo the top button while she lowers her head. It unfolds easily over her. There is her face, smooth skin, small but juicy lips, jet black hair, shoulder length, smelling clean, and shiny. Standing with arms to her sides, looking sideways, one reaches round to find the key to the restricting garment. Pull the small clasp together, it gives way, falling to the ground... joining its dormant friends. The firmness bounces slightly as the weight finds its seating, as dark brown nipples erect to a stiff firmness. She falls back onto the bed in slow motion, hair bouncing up and over her face. She lays there motionless, as if waiting for one to do just as one pleases, so one does.

Down on all fours over the top of her, move the face slowly over the smooth naked skin down to the now three garments left. Rub the nose gently over the stomach, down towards her crotch, reaching the bottom of the skirt. Hands push it up and over her hips... tights... nice!

Grab the front gusset and dig the fingers into the nylon material, slowly tearing them open to be confronted with more delightful obstacles.

The aroma of Surf Automatic, her red cotton underwear easily slides to one side with the help of calm fingers. The aroma of 'Shield' soap mists the fantastically shaped pubic hair zone, where the tongue dives in like a thirsty farmer.

Lapping like a dog after a long hot run, expertly opening her pussy lips with warm thumbs, engulfing the pussy like it's a meal to die for.

Hands move to firmly hold the underside of her legs at the knee joint, pushing them up in the air so as to get the face fully planted in the sodden garden of beauty. Juices flow, giving freedom to the internal, previously restricted. Sweet to the taste, the orgasm needs to engulf the facial mass. Swap positions, so she can control the tempo and pressure.

One's legs now over the end of the bed with feet planted firmly on the floor. She's crouching over the lapping frenzy, legs spread as far as they will go. Her pussy grinding into the nose in rhythm like a well oiled machine, stronger and faster it grinds.

A groaning growl starting to emerge from the depths of her throat indicates an orgasm in the making; it won't be long before the pussy goes into spasms. A hand clasps the penis...it's her twin!

She's standing directly over the rock hard unemployed penis. Yes she's going to... the warmth of the other twin's pussy envelopes the rock hard member, she sinks right down onto... a noisy sigh sounds out like a tension fully satisfied. NOW IT'S GOING ON!

One twin riding smoothly, rhythmically, the other grinding away with her pussy all over one's face.

The twin, forcing down her crouching groin, lets out a deep gurgling noise, her legs spasm like vibrating steel, she bounces uncontrollably on the face, neglecting, then uncaringly produces the full impact of what can only be described as a waterfall.

Slowly the waters subside along with long groans and whimpers from the owner.

Attention moves to the other. She's leant back, shouting and bouncing around like she's riding a space hopper... the shouting turns to groans with the rhythmic movements turning to slow soft shudders. The twins are out of breath, slumped all over me. They are heavy...

All I can hear is that stupid fucking 80s music, and see some lanky bloke who looks a little weird to say the least going through the card section next to me. His face is shiny. It doesn't look normal, not that I can see that much of it with his long greasy hear draped over it down to his nose... wanker.

As for the twins in front...if only they knew how much they enjoyed the last few minutes. I need to wipe my forehead as the heat of my mind has caused perspiration to occur...I'll just have to put up with it for the moment, or maybe someone would be good enough to find a hankie for me?...Anyway, now that I've got that off my chest, I can carry on with how the nutter gets on. I have to deal with things when they occur, you know how it is... So...

Chapter 27

The Villa, Part 1 - Shit or Bust

Up on his feet he turns, kicking up the sand with eyes now focused and mind in tune with professionalism. Mack makes his way up the slightly graduated beachfront and through the small collection of bars and shops. The relaxed attitude, ambience and voices of fun fade into a more sombre sound. The tarmac road that leads to the villa is now solid underfoot. Confirming that the deal has begun, Mack starts the short walk towards the target.

Either side of the road and beyond show that nature hasn't been cut down or mowed. Tall trees and undisturbed ground foliage provide the perfect natural camouflage. Using these natural obstacles to his utmost ability, he makes his way to the target and circles it for a 'recce.' Mack needs as much info from the surrounding area as he can get, he can then plot the escape route. Making sure the exit by the outhouse is still accessible, with no obvious obstructions, and this is confirmed. But, he also confirms that the only way into the villa is by the front doors, or by the outhouse. The outhouse isn't accessible from the outside, so he only has one way in, through those front doors.

Laying in the half sand and half-wiry grass, roughly a hundred yards from the glass wind breakers and getting comfortable, the binoculars become employed to survey the target. Lying flat on his belly and resting on his elbows he peers through the eyepieces. The front lounge comes into focus, but the fat man's not visible. However, the 4x4 the Turks use is, and it's parked on the drive. This means they're definitely in there. Mack needs confirmation that the fat man's there. He has the key to open the safe, and Mack *wants* those plates.

Sweat starts to soak his cap. The lenses around the eyepieces steam up, placing them down on the deck, a large swig of water and a breather brings his temperature to a norm.

A loud laugh comes from the villa. Mack puts the binoculars to his eyes. It's the fat man and he's in the lounge, talking loudly into a mobile phone as he waves his free arm around expressively. This is all the confirmation Mack needs for a strike; plotting his route, he starts his short and slow movements to get closer to the villa. Crawling through the scrub, he reaches a lower level of rocks just beneath the glass wind breakers. Again he's in spitting distance of the target.

Listening intently, the Turks can be heard talking. Mack takes the cap off his sweaty head slowly peeking over the top of the boulder. The Turks sit at the table drinking lemonade. The fat man walks around the lounge, still on the phone as he bursts into over exaggerated laughter every now and again, larging up his persona, totally oblivious to the carnage that will shortly follow. The villa seem very relaxed and off guard, which is exactly how Mack had wanted it.

This is the most dangerous part, he's got to get to the lounge fast enough so all three don't have time to react.
If he's slow, they'll have him, if he's fast but they see him too soon, then they'll still have him. He needs to get closer.
The element of surprised confusion should do it. They're not on their guard, this should be enough.

He has to let the phone call end, there's nothing like letting the whole world know what's going down as it happens. Slowly sliding his arms out of the rucksack, he tucks the binoculars in, takes the duck tape out and places it in his pocket, then waits... and waits.

Just over an hour later, Mack`s checking over the boulder, looking for an opportunity every minute or so. The fat man addresses Ennis, the elder of the Turks about the phone call. He talks loudly about a 'Farang' in Surat Thani buying certain products which not many tourists buy. They agree this would be Mack, which means he's probably on the island ready for a strike. *They're getting there.* Mack thinks with a grin.

The fat man orders Ennis to go into Thong Sala and find out from the tourist office and boat owners if any of them know of someone of Mack`s description being given a ride to the island, or to a guest place. Ennis slides his gun off the table tucking it into his waistband and makes his way to the 4x4. It roars off down the dusty lane. This only leaves Ally, the fat man, and the French hit-man wherever he is...if he's in there at all? Mack still watches the lounge intently.

The fat man disappears through the adjoining door and into the corridor.

*This is it!...*Mack quickly and quietly springs into action. His hand on top of the three foot glass wind breaker straddling it effortlessly without a sound. Carrying his body forward in momentum taking long steps on the balls of his feet he reaches the Turk who's sitting on the chair with his back showing. From behind, he puts his left hand round the Turk's chin, right hand on the back of his head, leans in, and in one sharp movement, jerks the Turk's head down and to the left. The strike is so hard that the Turk almost looks backwards, which gives Mack a glimpse of the look in Ally's eyes, as his head violently twists. Fear, surprise, and a knowing look of death that's only ever seen with this manoeuvre. Snap! The Turk's neck is broken, his arms fly outwards and upwards as the nerves give the last command, and then he sits there, chin on chest, limp... body jolting as if from an electric shock.

Mack pulls the Kimber from Ally's front trouser belt. Flicking the mag out, he checks it, live rounds are there, and judging by its weight...probably full, then flicks the safety catch off.

Moving fast to the wall beside the door to the corridor, Mack stands back flat to it with the gun at shoulder height, pointing across the doorway, ready for anything. He widens his mouth so any heavy breathing from his last manoeuvres escape with minimal sound, and waits for the return of the fat man.

A door from the corridor closes with a hollow echo. Two seconds later the sweaty mass of the fat man wanders through not noticing the intruder flat against the wall. Mack grabs him round the neck shoving the Kimber into his ear. The fat man would know this is very real, by the hardness and temperature of the steel.

"You move, you die" Mack whispers with hot breath into his ear, kissing the gun.

The fat man not only knows he's in trouble, but looking at the table he can see that Ally's either unconscious, or dead, this confirms the seriousness of what's going on.

"Okay, Okay," he croaks, struggling to breathe.

"Get the fuck down on your knees, and put your arms and hands behind your back!" Mack demands quietly spitting through his teeth.

The fat man does as he's told while the Kimber's nozzle moves from his ear, to the back of his neck.
Mack digs into his thigh pocket retrieving the duck tape. Slowly tearing a piece off with his teeth, he tapes the fat man's mouth, then wraps it round his hands, wrists, and as far up his arms as it will go.

"Move to the chair" Mack says, now totally in control.

Clumsily he gets up as his weight and restrictions seem difficult to handle, and quietly moves to the chair. Mack pulls his taped up arms up his back slightly so the fat man's bent over in pain with thoughts of what's might happen next, as the Kimber presses uncomfortably into the back of his sweaty head. Mack moves a chair to the corner of the table turning it round.

"Sit down," he commands in a whisper.

The overweight lump dejectedly flops down on the chair. Mack tapes his legs to the chair legs, puts his arms behind the back of the chair, and then tapes the back chair legs to the table leg with his arms stuck between the chair and table. No way is the lump going to move from there. The first part of the hit has been without incident. He now has to check the rest of the building, locate the hit man, and take him out.

Mack knows the hit man's ex foreign legion and Special Forces, so he'll be as well trained as himself. No injuries have been sustained so far, and he's only used minimal energy...he's ready.

The corridor shows no light. The doors are only just visible. The first door on the left is where the safe is, four more doors, two on the right, one further up on the left, and the door at the end. Mack needs to know where the hit man is...that's if he's there at all. Returning to the fat man and kneeling down, he looks directly into the his eyes...

"I want to know where Christophe` is."

The fat man makes a noise while nodding his head towards the corridor and the other bedrooms.

"Shhhhh." Mack quietly exclaims, putting a finger to his mouth.
"In one of the bedrooms?" The fat man nods.
"Asleep?" The fat man nods again.
"Okay, I want *you* to call out to Christophe` as if you have something to tell him...Okay? Now...I'm going to take this tape off your mouth, if you let him know I'm here, I'll shoot you in the bollocks, and you'll have a very slow and painful death, so do as I say...Okay?"

The fat man nods fast and makes an urgent, "mmm, mmm" sound. Mack takes this as a 'yes' by the look of agreement in his eyes. His face contorts with pain as the tape comes off.

"Okay, now call him." Mack says in a cool, calm voice.
"Christophe!... Christophe!" he shouts in exactly the tone Mack wanted.
"Again."   Mack   commands.
"Christophe, Christophe!" he shouts again a little louder this time.

A sleepy grunt is clearly heard coming from one of the rooms. Quickly Mack replaces the tape over the fat man's mouth, then bounds effortlessly without a sound across the tiled floor to the doorway leading to the hallway. Standing back to the wall again, Kimber ready...he waits.

Chapter 28

The Villa, Part 2 – Christophe'

And waits... nothing. Crouching down, knees cracking, he hopes he hasn't given his position away by sound of his joints disagreeing with his movement . Manoeuvring himself quietly, he lays down on the tiled floor ready to pop his head round the bottom of the door, Kimber ready and checking the safety catch again....

In a swift movement he pokes his head and gun round the door aiming where he anticipates the hit man to be... no target.
Shit!... where is he?
Quietly, keeping low Mack returns to the fat man and asks...
"What room's he in? Now, I will hold up my left hand for the left side. Mack holds his hand up.
"Yes or no?" The fat man shakes his head no.
"Nod once for the first door or twice for the second door." He nods twice.

Moving stealthily towards the door to the second bedroom on the right, he presses himself up against the wall, resting by the handle. Mack has to make a decision; does he smash through the door, creating as much confusion to the now half-awake Christophe hoping for the element of surprise? Alternatively...take the softly-softly approach?

This could go either way. If I smash in the door he could be waiting, so take me out on my blind entrance, and if I go softly he could also be waiting.

Mack tries the door handle...it turns, then clicks. The door opens a millimetre or so. Slowly pushing it open, still with his back to the wall, it slowly swings opens fully stopping with a slight clonk...nothing. Mack can see no light, its dark, and quiet. He doesn't like this, he's got to enter the room, a dark room where a well trained assassin is either sleeping, or waiting to do the business.

The choices are immediately answered by the gentle sound of clothing rubbing together behind him. Mack turn his head...he's now looking down the barrel of a SIG P228. The long muscular arm belongs to an unshaven dark haired hit man, who's looking at Mack with eyes wide, holding an expression of death on his worn and tanned face.

Stupid twat! How could I have been so sloppy? He must have heard me unrolling the duck tape; I made no other noise. Mack curses to himself. *Don't even wait for further instructions from the opponent, move, and move fast!*

In lightning movements, ducking and spinning out of the firing line of the SIG P228, Mack brings his leg up going for the snap kick to the groin and a knife strike to Christophe's gun hand. The knife strike solidly finds its target, dislodging the SIG from Christophe's grip, making the gun fall to the floor, but the kick's blocked by a knee...and a hard fist smashes into Mack's jaw.

Mack's adrenalin takes care of any pain while he points his gun at the large powerful torso of Christophe`. Wham! Christophe's foot comes in with such force that Mack's hand and gun smash against the wall, removing the gun from his hand crashing the Kimber to the floor with the sound of metal on tile, echoing.
Both guns are on the floor now. Punches, feet, knees, heads, elbows, knife strikes, all coming at once, there's more blocks and strikes than Mack or Christophe can cope with.

Feeling confident that he has the advantage, as he can clearly see Christophe's silhouette from the light behind, Mack tries to keep his attacks on the inside, however, Christophe` can clearly see Mack too, because of the light shining on him from behind Christophe`, Mack decides he doesn't have the advantage at all, so needs another angle.
Dropping to the floor he smashes his right foot into Christophe's calves with such force that Christophe's legs leave the floor by two or three feet landing him awkwardly in a crumpled mass, his eyes fixed on Mack. Christophe` waits for the next manoeuvre trying to curl up knowing he's totally open to attack. Mack aims for the groin with his foot, blocked by Christophe's knee. Again like a piston Mack goes for the groin, again not connecting.

A heel kick connects to Christophe's thigh spinning him round to be side on. Christophe grapples around for Mack's legs grabbing his foot, going for the break. Mack spins himself out of the grip landing himself on the floor administering a powerful back-fist blow to the side of Christophe`s head.

Side by side in the slim hallway they try pounding each other going for the advantage, arm strikes, legs and hand strikes, all trying to connect as they swim around on the glazed tiles, some blows finding their target, some not. Mack can feel Christophe's powerful arms lock around his neck in the death grip, he knows if he doesn't break this, he'll be out in about anywhere between three and ten seconds, Mack has to break this hold.

Christophe's legs aren't wrapped round the midsection for a full on hold, giving Mack a chance, his only chance. Firmly planting his feet on the corridor wall and mustering as much strength as he has left from his failing consciousness, he pushes their squirming bodies in a circular fashion. Christophe's legs get awkwardly stuck against the wall. Pushing with failing power but twisting at the same time, Mack lands a sharp elbow straight into Christophe's ribs, twisting the now red face and head from the death lock.

With a small distance now between them, they quickly clamber to their feet while relentlessly like oiled machines still go for the strikes and blocks. Mack lunges at Christophe sprawling them out into the lounge in a wrestling match. Freeing themselves from the tussle and both needing space, they clamber to their knees, trying to find some balance.

Mack gets a glimpse of the fat man pushing and pulling at his restraints, willing Christophe on, wanting Mack dead.

If only he could have seen how the fight was going a few seconds ago, that would have given him some confidence in being released from his restraints, by a man on his own side.

Back-fists and elbows still trying to connect from both parties trying desperately for the upper hand, power and accuracy pump in at wild force that would stop most people immediately, but not these two, these two are trained for this, this is a fight that would open the eyes of a Mu Thai champion.

Mack drops his shoulder to the ground while thrusting his heel into Christophe's face connecting well. Christophe absorbs the kick sliding backwards into the low lounge coffee table. Mack tries to take advantage while Christophe`s off balance, lunging for the neck. Christophe's feet plant perfectly on Mack's chest throwing him over in an acrobatic somersault, landing him on his back the other side of the table, half in and half out of the lounge and onto the balcony. Christophe goes for the same move diving for Mack's neck. Mack doesn't have time to raise his legs to copy the manoeuvre, but his knees break Christophe's attack while turning him over onto Mack's right hand side.

Again, both striking while clambering up, Mack catches Christophe's hand while on a palm strike bending it back on itself, going for the wrist break. Christophe anticipates the move pulling Mack onto him while again falling backwards and tossing Mack over into a somersault. Mack flies past Ally's paralysed body landing hard on his back. Quickly he jumps up turning with a jumping spinning round house kick to where he anticipates Christophe's` face to be, but Christophe` hadn`t reached him yet. With Mack's foot landing Christophe`s already coming in with a front kick of his own, looking for a solid connection. Mack catches Christophe's foot, and using Christophe`s own forward momentum he manages to pull him forward while turning him and smashing his torso into the kitchen work surface. Christophe` opens a drawer fumbling around inside it while fending off another knee shattering kick from Mack. Grabbing the biggest knife in the drawer and in a sweeping circular motion the knife slices Mack on the inside of his right forearm, opening a wound that spurts blood in a line diagonally up Christophe's chest and on to the ceiling. Mack, trying to evade any other strikes, spirals along the work surface towards where the fat man's tied up. Grabbing a magazine at the far end of the work surface he quickly rolls it into a solid tube shape while moving backwards, just in time to block another knife attack while kicking Christophe in the gut and stopping him in his tracks, putting some space between them.

For a split second they stand there, legs apart, arms outstretched, leaning towards each other, Mack bleeding badly with the rolled up magazine in his right hand and Christophe with the knife in his right hand. They both pant like a couple of worn out bulls at a bull fight.

Eyeing each other, what moves could they do next to out manoeuvre the other? Mack composes himself, regaining a focal point, moving himself into a knife-hand back-stance position, ignoring his wound, which is pumping out life's fluids down his arm, he knows he'll have to do something soon, as the blood loss will start taking its toll.

Christophe makes the move...he lunges forward leading with his left leg, both hands coming across his body towards Mack's face, *He's going for the kill!*

Anticipating Christophe's intentions with the knife, Mack makes his move too. He drops the magazine, and in one fluid huge last effort, just as Christophe's nearly on top of him, he grabs both Christophe's wrists, then moves in with his right shoulder, tucks it into Christophe's chest, bends the knees absorbing Christophe's weight, and transfers the forwarding momentum back on itself using an aikido manoeuvre. He then pulls backwards on Christophe's wrists with all the strength he has, the force of this counter attack sends Christophe into an uncontrolled on-the-spot somersault, landing him smack on his back. Mack still has hold of Christophe's wrists, which are now bent back causing excruciating pain.

Using his own dead weight, he drops onto Christophe's chest cavity pulling on the knife, which is now pointing towards Christophe's throat, inwards, Mack pulls, as hard as he can. Christophe stops the knife just before it enters. It's now a struggle of strength, and Mack has the edge, he has the higher ground, he has his bodyweight behind him, he wants the knife in Christophe's neck... Christophe` doesn't.

With what energy they have left, grunts and shouts escape from both of their mouths, pushing and pulling against each other's fading power. Slowly but surely the knife gets closer to Christophe's neck. Christophe`, knowing that this could be his last effort, makes a last grunting fight to push the knife away while thrashing his body and legs in the air, trying to break Mack's hold...to no avail.

Mack's hold is not going to fade, his strength is not going to fade, his focus is not going to fade. The knife slowly eases into Christophe's neck. First the tip that breaks the skin, then a little further which cuts a vein, then, with one last pull, the whole blade slides in. Blood gushes from his neck like a pumping generator. Mack holds him there as Christophe` squirms and gurgling sounds ooze from a gaping wound, as blood and air escape from places it shouldn't. Mack holds him tighter as the fight gets easier, knowing it won't be long, just long enough for it to take, to take for his body to stop moving...which it does.

Mack relaxes his overworked muscles, letting go of Christophe's dead hand, and slowly gets off the blood soaked carcass. Kneeling where he is, panting like a dog, he looks at the body with the pool of blood covering a large area of the tiled floor around it. He almost feels sad. Mack had great respect for this fighter, they had a common bond. It's always a shame to see such training and expertise go to waste. However...it was to the death, they both knew it, and Christophe' lost. Mack knows it will be his turn to lose one day too, but today isn't that day, not by the hands of this chap anyway.

Mack's absolutely knackered, and doesn't want another fight like that for a while. The swelling and throbbing coming from his face lets him know he's had a good work out. His chest hurts, his back hurts, his hand hurts, his legs and arms hurt from all the blocks and strikes, in fact he's pretty well beaten up, and a certain knife wound to the forearm needs attending to.

Finding his tired feet, Mack slowly gets up from his aching knees, one foot after the other. Washing his arms and hands from the body's life liquid under the tap while looking at the fat man, he ties his arm with a tea towel to stem the flow, not taking his eyes off him. Mack flicks his eyes to the dead carcass on the floor and back to the sweaty live stench of fear glowing on the fat man's face, it's all too apparent.
Mack knows he'll do anything now to save his own crime ridden skin, which is good, because he needs the key and combination to get into the safe. Mack could go home now, in all honesty the hit man's been taken care of, so the money's in the can. However, the plates will bring a good bonus, not only that, there's a score to settle...from back in Chaing Mai.

Pulling the tape from the fat man's mouth, he asks where the first aid box is. The fat man's only too glad to help, spurting out that it's under the sink cupboard.

"Where... is the key to the safe?" Mack asks, as he calmly looks for a sewing needle. Mack's secretly impressed with the first aid box, he's found a curved sowing needle, and not only that, some fibre thread to stitch himself up with. Looking at the fat man while sewing the pumping gash, he asks again,...."Where is the key to the safe?"

"They're in the 4x4 that Ennis is using." the fat man says, knowing that Mack won't be happy with this reply. Mack looks at him in disbelief...

"Oh... for fuuuck's sake... you're having a laugh ain't ya?"

"No, they really are, I promise." He returns, being as helpful as possible, thinking that if the nutter gets the plates he'll leave, and spare the miserable life of the fat man.

Biting the fibre off from his arm, he dresses the stitches with a large sticky plaster while walking to the corridor and picking up the guns. Returning and placing them on the table by the now seriously sweaty lump of a sad man, he pulls a chair from underneath, sitting on it dejectedly; Mack looks at the fat man and repeats his unhappy reply.

"For fuuuuck's sake!" then looks at the ceiling, breathing out heavily.

Chapter 29

The Villa, Part 3 – Goodbye

The 4x4 slides abruptly to a halt on the parquet stone driveway. The vehicles door slams shut, giving Mack an indication that he has about five seconds to get into an offensive position. Grabbing the Kimber from the table while finding some energy and grimacing with pain, he speedily sprints to the large French windows, flattening himself up against the lounge wall, again waiting.

Ennis walks through the French doors. Before he can react to the scene that greets him of post pandemonium, he's grabbed around the neck from behind. Mack pushes the cold steel of the gun into his neck.

"Sit down Ennis." Mack says in an "it's going to be okay." tone to calm him.

Ennis moves to the chair next to his brother and sits. Looking at his brother he starts to quietly sob as the realisation of his brother's limp body slumped over the table with his head holding the body up in an awkward looking position, brings it home, hard. Christophe's dead body in the pool of blood can be seen from where Ennis sits. The realisation and scale of what's occurred while he's been away hits him like a hammer, the fatmans taped up and whimpering body slams to clarity...this could also be the last entry on *his* CV.

Mack takes the duck tape wrapping it round Ennis's arms like he did with the fat man.

"Now," Mack says calmly, "where, in the 4x4, are the keys to the safe?"

Ennis's shoulders are bouncing uncontrollably by this time, his sobs tell a million stories of pain and loss, memories of his childhood with Ally and his parents flood his mind, but now with grief. Ally was the youngest, it was Ennis`s job...his job to look after his brother, see that no real harm came to him...and now...he looks now at a lifeless body. Speaking through his high pitched whimpers, he says quietly,

"If it's the keys to the safe you want, then they're in my left hand pocket."

Without emotion Mack slides a hand in his jeans pocket pulling out the keys and saying a thank you. Looking at them while walking over to the fat man, he pulls the tape off.

"Okay, what's the code?" he asks looking the lump straight in the eye.
"0836, then press enter. The green light will come on, then insert the key and turn clockwise." he replies wanting Mack to take what he wants and go without killing him, or Ennis.

After all the tricks the fat man's pulled in the past, Mack hopes the safe isn't rigged. It's a chance he has to take, but sounds the fat man out.

"Under this table are plastic explosives ready to go off in ten minutes. If the safe's rigged, I won't be back to turn them off, and you die. So if it's rigged you better tell me now." Mack says while arming the devices in full view, so they know he's serious.

"No honestly, it's just a safe, nothing else." he replies sounding sincere.

Mack goes to the safe. Pulling up the rug, he then opens the silver steel flap and punching in the code 0836, then presses enter. Pausing for a second he says a goodbye before turning clockwise. The safe lid pops up slightly.
Grabbing the swivel handle, he opens it to find various amounts of drugs, money, and a rolled up piece of cloth. Mack guesses that these are the plates. He takes the cloth bundle out, it's heavier than he remembered. Walking with the rolled fabric in his hands to the lounge, he puts it on the table, stops, and looks at the fat man while slowly unwrapping the hard objects.

Hoo-fuckin-rah.

The shiny silver 50 Euro plates are looking a little good in the bright midday light. To *his* eye, they look finished. Mack knows it's time to leave.

Pulling a chair up and leaning back, Mack breathes out as if the job's done. He looks the fat man in the eyes...and starts his speech.

"None of this need have happened if *you,* hadn't tried to stitch me up in Chang Mai...if *you,* had left me alone and not tried to be the big boss, *I* wouldn't be here today. We were only after Christophe, only to capture him...not kill him. You probably knew there's a bounty on his head. That's all we were trying to do, collect the bounty. *You* fucked all this up. *I* didn't want to kill anyone... *you...* made this happen." Mack says this with heavy regret in his voice.

He watches the fat man as the reality of today's proceedings sink in, turning him into a child wanting his mommy. He looks at the dead body of Christophe`, and then tries to look round to the paralysed lump of Ally. He knows this has been catastrophic, and he now knows it's all *his* fault. Playing gangster is one thing, but playing with someone like Mack...is something else.

Mack calmly rises from the chair, knowing the last steps of the job. The beauty of the world embraces him like a wash of freezing cold water, cleansing him as he walks through doors to free himself from this havoc. The locally innocent surroundings greet him, giving the free and fresh warm air as a token of its purity. Hot welcoming sun and the ambience of this beautiful island bring him back to normality, making his conscience tingle with humanity, but yet again, the job overpowers his conscience, giving way to professionalism. He ponders hard, wondering if he could get away with just leaving with the plates, but again his future dictates otherwise...Mack wants no repercussions, and there's only one way to make sure of that.

Standing for a second, he breathes out spotting some gulls that swoop down to feed from the glistening ocean, excitedly crying as they catch a fish and play. Warm fresh breezes caress his swollen face as he looks up at the bluest of blue skies. Mack looks down to the earlier discarded rucksack.

The day a rucksack like this holds a pair of trainers, a towel, and a tennis racket will be my finest.

Picking up the rucksack up from behind the glass wind breaker and rock, Mack wanders back to the lounge putting the rucksack heavily on the table, he unclicks the clasps, and gets out the detonators.

Ennis starts shouting, begging and crying. The begs turn again to whimpers, as if he's been convicted of a crime he never committed...and he didn't...the *fat man* did. Mack's mind doesn't feel the emotions that Ennis does, he's not the one who's about to be blown to smithereens, but if it was him in Ennis's position, he would be saying his goodbyes, and looking forward to meeting up with the friends that have gone before him.

The explosion distracts him from the smooth sound of wind rushing past his ears as the Bayliner carves a route back to Surat Thani. Turning, he watches as flames shoot through the windows. Another loud explosion that must have been the gas mains produces a scene of carnage, like something out of a film, a mushroom-shaped fire ball bellows into the picturesque backdrop. Mack watches contentedly as the flames dissipate into the trees canopies. Another explosion follows, bricks and wood shoot high into the blue creating another scene of devastation.

Mack's always intrigued by the unsynchronised sound and sight phenomenon that happens when watching explosions from a distance. He won't be needing that number the chap gave him yesterday for...a ride home

***

Well, that's what I heard about him anyway. As for the alien shit, to be honest I have no fucking idea what he's on about. However, I wouldn't want to be on the receiving end of him, not that I ever would be.

Fuck me! I still want that piss... badly! Thank fuck we've only got those stupid fat wankers, and a couple of others to go before I get served. The wheels are turning, and need to be turning faster. Now it's the turn of the fat prats.

Chapter 30

A Robbery

Before they have a chance to meander themselves to the window, shouting starts from behind me. The venue goes quiet as people's attention's drawn towards the shouting.

"GET DOWN ON THE FLOOR...NOW!" the explosive voice demands. Clearly confused, people slowly begin to do as they're told, while looking around as if some sort of director of a film set is going to turn up at any minute shouting "Cut!"

It doesn't happen.

"GET THE FUCK DOWN AND DON'T MOVE!" the voice shouts again.

This time with squeals of fear, confusion and the realisation, people's actions speed up tenfold as they drop to the floor. To the other side of me at the counter window I see a man wearing glasses and a bobble hat. He holds a knife up at the window, he shouts loudly at the server to put money into a plastic Sainsbury's bag that he's thrusting under the counter window. The attendant who wore the condescending expression earlier, is only too happy to oblige as she grabs money from the drawer and stuffs the notes into the bag as fast as she can, looking like she's just wet herself with terror.

"FASTER, YOU BITCH!" The man pushes his face up to the window, which no doubt makes a great picture on the CCTV.

The man at the back of the room also shouts his commands for people to stay down and not to move. Adrenalin pumps like a well-oiled piston through my heart, pounding my head in painful awareness of the situation. My body's jerking uncontrollably in anger and panic. Trudy makes a slight move, bringing her face up to see how things are, giving the man from the back a reason to leap over to her and land the blunt end of an eight inch bone handle sheath knife straight down on her head. Her face bounces off the floor in unconsciousness, as an explosion of deep red blood spurts from her skull, landing on the twins who are holding each other, protecting each other, comforting each other.

Blood on clothes and skin give rise to more squeals, screams, and a man's terror of the deep vocal shock. It couldn't have happened to a nicer person, as I realise these people aren't to be messed with. I think most people have come to that conclusion too. There's no sound, no one moves, the blood and pain hangs like from a torturer waiting to go to work...

The plastic bag's now full of notes and the drawers are empty. Grabbing the bag the bobble hat man shouts,

"GO-GO-GO!" as he starts his long sprint over the body strewn floor. A black crombie coated man erupts from floor, jumping to waist height while landing a sickening thud with his fist bang on target...the bobble hat man's groin.

A pathetic high-pitched screech leaves his screwed up face as he doubles up on the floor, meeting his captives in immense pain. His accomplice tries to help the now curled up lump. Trying quickly to make his way over, he's met with Geezer grabbing at the jeans that he tries so hard to weave through the carnage. He stumbles, providing a clear and waiting advantage to be had, advantage to Mack. Bam!..the heel of a polished loafer connects to the stumbling jaw forcing the contorted face to almost say goodbye to its neck... skyward. He falls on top of his accomplice in a heap.

You could have heard a pin drop as their dead weights show defeat from the hands of the local heroes. Mack checks Trudy's wound while shouting to a stunned and wide-eyed staff to phone the police, ambulance, and to get a cloth. Geezer`s also shouting to the staff to get some cable ties, or something to tie the robber's hands. The staff and customers spring into action, darting around, some chasing their own tail in panic, some with phones to their ears, and some passing drying up cloths from the tea room over to stem the blood. Shock settles in. It all seems like the aftermath of a bombing raid as the venue seems to slow into a more organised fracas.

With job done, Mack leaves the premises. Geezer waits for the police to turn up, then he can claim his righteous pat on the back, and have his picture taken for the local rag. I just wish I could have done something...but it was all taken care of.

We stay until the idiots have been handcuffed and laid onto stretchers. Everyone makes a statement, telling of a local hero that left the building. As normality slowly returns, we can now get on with what we came here to do in the first place. The premises don't even close, because the other half of the service counter didn't get robbed, which makes me very happy...because I just want to get served and get down the fucking pub, and have that piss.

Chapter 31

The Tenants

'Topper', everyone calls him, (his nickname because he tries to top what everyone else has done) now moves to the counter with his manky sweaty wife in tow. His T-shirt shows some sort of a Scottish football team logo, which protrudes massively out and over his beech ball of a greedy stomach. His manky overweight miserable wife stands next to him, her face up against the window peering in intimidatingly. Her seriously out of shape, overweight arse sticks out like she's trying to look sexy, but not quite understanding that everyone sees her for what she is, ugly and overweight.

I hear him ask for a car tax form. Why would anyone want to put tax on a poxy small front wheel drive look-alike jeep? They must have to actually prize themselves into it, and when they get in, how they have room to operate anything is a miracle on its own. I reckon they're trying to make themselves look physically smaller, stupid twats.

The trouble with these two is simple. They took over the local boozer a couple of weeks ago. In those two weeks, they've managed to bar all the locals. Their reasons for the Barings range from the ridiculous, to the damn right fucking ridiculous. Everyone thinks they were 'trying to make their mark'...very much the wrong way to go about it in my mind.

No one I've heard of likes them, and they're so far up their own arses they don't like anyone else either. The truth be known, they don't like each other, or even themselves, fucking idiots.

The other day, while I was admiring the view of a few scantily clad dressed young ladies and taking a sip from my drink, the arrogant twit of a landlady brashly walked over to one of the locals (who's been drinking in the pub for over twenty years) and accused him of being drunk.

The look on his face was of total disbelief, he couldn't believe what he was hearing. In fact, I think I remember him putting his finger in his ear and giving it a wiggle to see if his hearing all right.

He honestly tells her, that it's only his second pint. She reckoned he'd been drinking elsewhere beforehand. A chat starts between them, with the local getting more irate by the second. Jan (that's her name) slowly begins to realise that it's *she* who's the one that's out of order, *she's* the one who's in the wrong, which is bad news, because the last thing this idiot of a woman wants, is to look bad in front of her customers.

However, Jan being Jan, she then demands that he leaves the establishment immediately. She does this by screaming at the top of her voice so as to embarrass him, hoping that he'll leave quickly as a consequence. (It normally works)
Of course the local's extremely pissed off about this. He stands up to her and demands his money back for the pint he hasn't finished.

With this she carries on screaming at him to get out or she'll call the police. Slowly his facial expression changes into a very serious look. Looking her in the eye, he points a finger at her and calmly says,

"You're out of order."

And without taking his eyes off her, he downs his drink in a second or two and leaves. As he's leaving she shouts at him,

"You're barred!" He stops in his tracks, pausing for a moment, looks around and says,

"For what?"
She says nothing, just turns and walks behind the bar like she's King fucking Kong, and just stopped a murder going down or something, and she's now some sort of hero. He turns back round to the exit, and calmly walks out the doors.

The evening's din of noise returns to its normal level, with most of the conversation around me of about how the chap had just been badly mistreated by this manky landlady. Listening to a group behind me, I hear one of them say they've known the chap for years, and there's no way he would let anyone treat him like that. 'He's a bit of a loose cannon.'

Of course I happen to know his past to, and they're right, he is a loose cannon, so I didn't think that was the last we were going to see or hear from him either.

Half an hour later...Crack! I turn my eyes towards the bar. I see a person standing there with a full face balaclava on. I almost laugh. He's holding up a cricket bat and has just whacked it on the bar top making all the drinks jump up, spilling and smashing. Glass and booze everywhere. Nothing verbally comes from his mouth, and then pandemonium...swinging that bat as if he's hitting a fast bowl for six, smashing everything in sight.

Everyone's running, frantically moving to the perimeters of the boozer taking tables and chairs with them in the rush, shielding themselves from the flying debris. Once the main bar itself was empty of anything else to smash, he walked casually behind the bar and started smashing all the optics, bottles, shelves, anything that was there. I remember seeing a pair of metal ice tongs fly through the air, almost in slow motion, embedding themselves in the softwood optics shelf, twanging a little.
Within a minute he'd transformed the back bar to resemble a derelict pub, he just went mental. *She,* had disappeared, but I remember hearing her screaming. (probably down the phone to the police).
"The pub's being smashed up! The pub's being smashed up!!!"

That's all you could hear, because the whole place had descended into a shocked silence. He stood there looking around for anyone to do something...no one did. The next thing, he goes to where the screams were coming from...then it went quite. We all thought he'd murdered her (which I feel a lot of people wouldn't have objected to.) The next thing we hear is...

"I'm fucking barred am I?!!! Well, now I've fucked your bar!!... Okay!!! That makes us quits... O-fucking-kay!"

He came out from where the shouting was and just...walked out the door, no one did fuck all, in fact I'm sure I saw someone clapping.

The police turned up about an hour later. We all knew it was him, but because he was wearing the balaclava, and had a solid alibi for where he was at the time of the incident, he got away with it. It serves the stupid wankers right.

I did hear though that someone in the boozer grassed him up, but without giving a full name. They didn't think it was *really* grassing because they didn't give the full name. I think they missed out a letter of his surname, but as far as I know they got the address right. Fucking pussy arse grasses!

But here they are, the big fat tenants, in this waiting queue, acting cock-a-hoop, talking to the staff like they own the village, absolute wankers.

Well today I've seen 'em all, the twins, Geezer, the dodgy one, the psycho and now the tenant fat bastards. The place has been robbed, I've had a great shag with the twins, and now it's my turn to be served.

***

We're now leaving this shit-hole of a post office, making our way over the road and up the high street to the pub. I can have that piss now...empty my catheter bag.

We've arrived at the pub, and I'm sitting in my usual corner, looking out as usual, with my pint wedged between my dysfunctional hands, supping away through my straw, they know I still like a pint.
Yeah I've seen myself in the mirror, teeth grinning like a fucked up leper, trying to talk to them, but only achieving unrecognisable grunts, squeals and jerky body movements...It winds me up even more.

Everyone in the boozer says hello to me like I'm a child. It's a shame I can't tell them all to fuck off because they're all a bunch of wankers.

You see, being a quadriplegic from the neck down. I can't do much except take in the outside world, make my own assumptions, and watch everyone else go about their business.

But hey, that's what you get for being drunk, and diving into the shallow end of a swimming pool, at 41 years old on a family holiday. Not only did my spinal cord snap, but because I effectively drowned, I suffered brain damage too, so I can`t even talk for fuck sake. Mind you, I get to watch my helpers shagging each other when they think they can get away with it. They think I don't watch, (a quickie they call it)...just wish I could join in...or at least have a wank, bastards!...And you wonder why I'm so fucking angry... Fuck off!

Chapter 32:   Thank god for goodbye`s

The tiredness I feel, sitting confined within myself, and this mobile chair with rubber and metal spindles, leather harnesses and a carbon frame, grows like a warm shroud, comforting me as my rolling eyes can`t stay focused, supping through my straw becomes impossible.

My head weighs in like a lead balloon, ready to crash into my lap, connected, but hanging on the end of a rubber neck with no energy to move, my mind starts to wander, am I waking?

My legs...I can *feel* my legs, my shoulders, I'm rolling them, my toes...are they them that I can really feel move? Blood warms as it makes its way through body's inners...life's fluid flows again...I feel strong, am I waking?

The entrance door throbs brighter by the second...a white light splays, overriding any other sight, all occupants seem to disappear, sounds fade into silence, I am waking.

I don`t feel afraid...no more fear, feelings of bitterness...I feel no more. An overwhelming wash of calm, an invite...a presence...

I am rising...

I am awake.